The Book of Sports Lists #2

It started out as a game. Any number could play. It was called list-making. Before we knew it, a book had emerged: *The Book of Sports Lists*. And now, by popular demand, and because we are compulsive list-makers, there is *The Book of Sports Lists #2.*

The attributed lists are authentic. Others are the brainchildren of the editors. We thank those who responded to our request for lists, and we apologize to those whose lists did not make it.

We hope that our lists will grow and that there will be *The Book of Sports Lists #3* (we're going to keep doing it until we do it right). We invite you, the reader, to participate. Send your list to:

Associated Features
370 Lexington Avenue
New York, NY 10017

Do it today. Don't delay. Put it at the top of your list.

Also by Phil Pepe and Zander Hollander:
The Book of Sports Lists

THE BOOK OF SPORTS LISTS #2

BY PHIL PEPE AND
ZANDER HOLLANDER

An Associated Features Book
PINNACLE BOOKS LOS ANGELES

1 Outstanding Person, Who Has Educated, Encouraged, Counseled, Befriended, and Aided the Editors Through the Years, and to Whom This Book Is Dedicated

1. Herman L. Masin

EDITORS' NOTE: This list is alphabetical and not necessarily in order of preference.

THE BOOK OF SPORTS LISTS #2

An original Pinnacle Books edition, published for the first time anywhere.

First printing, June 1980

ISBN: O-523-40853-6

Cover illustration by Len Berzofsky

Printed in the United States of America

PINNACLE BOOKS, INC.
2029 Century Park East
Los Angeles, California 90067

Contents

1 THE WAY IT WAS 1

King Tut's 10 Favorite Sports 1
Ray Fitzgerald's 10 Vanishing Americanisms in Sport 2
Jerry Green's 17 Favorite Professional Teams That No Longer Exist 3
10 Obsolete Olympic Events That Would Be Nice to See Again 6
George Gipe's 20 Favorite Old-Time Major League Baseball Teams with Unusual Nicknames 6
George Gipe's 10 Favorite Old-Time Professional Football Teams with Unusual Nicknames 7

II ARTS AND LEISURE 9

Tom Gunderson's 10 Geatest Roller Coasters 9
George Kolombatovich's 10 Greatest Opera Duels 10
Herman L. Masin's 29 Prize-Winning Book Titles That Were Just Dying for a Designated Writer 11
Harvey Sabinson's 15 Musicals or Plays Rewritten for Bowie Kuhn 12
Don Dunphy's 10 Favorite Boxing Movies 15
10 Hollywood Movies with a Hockey Theme 17
Jack Keane's 12 Greatest Movie Fencers 18

III PLAY BALL 21

Joe DiMaggio's 4 Greatest Highlights of His Career 21
Joel Stein's 11 Best Letters from Baseball's All-Time Old-Timers 23
Bill Madden's 10 Most Valuable Baseball Cards 28
Dr. Frances A. Bock's 54 Tobacco Chewers and Their Idiosyncracies 31
Moss Klein's 11 Most Memorable (Publicized?) Yankee Controversies, 1977–79 32
Furman Bisher's 10 All-Time Baseball Holdouts 36
Red Foley's 10 Baseball Records That Will Never Be Broken 39
Billy Martin's 2 Commandments on How to Keep the Boss Happy 40
6 Active Baseball Players Who Are Locks for the Hall of Fame 41
14 Reference Books Without Which a Baseball Library Would Be Incomplete 42
Mel Allen's All-Time Team 43
The 10 Worst Teams in Baseball History 45

IV FIRST AND TEN 47

Buddy Young's 26 Fastest Backs and 1 Fastest Defensive Lineman of All Time 47
The 6 Commandments of the Church of Monday Night Football 50
Dave Jennings' 11 Biggest Kicking Plays in the NFL Over the Last 25 Years 51
John Steadman's Ratings for 14 Super Bowls 57
Mickey Herskowitz's 8 Worst No. 1 Picks in the Pro Football Draft 59
Allie Sherman's 10 Left-handed Quarterbacks 59
George Halas' 9 Essentials for Winning 61
Bum Phillips' 7 Rules for Coaching 45 Large Men 63
Herman L. Masin's 13 Most Meaningful Innovations in Football History 64
Ted Emery's All-Time Gator Bowl Team 64

V SAY IT AIN'T SO *67*

Jerry Coleman's 14 Best (But Not Only) Malaprops *67*
Ted Patterson's 8 Famous and Not So Famous Sportscasters' Bloopers *68*
17 One-to-Five Liners That Are Hanging Around Out There Waiting to Be Said *71*
Harold Rosenthal's 10 Most Memorable Baseball Quotes *73*
Red Holzman's 6 Basic Rules on Life *75*
John Halligan's 5 Favorite Hockey Quotes *75*
Graig Nettles' 7 Best One-Liners *77*
10 Quotations from Chairman Fred Shero *77*
5 Comments by Sports Figures, Having to Do with the Meaning of Life *78*

VI FORE! *79*

Arnold Palmer's Best 18 Golf Holes *79*
Joe Schwendeman's 10 Most and Memorable Holes-in-One *80*
The 10 Greatest Golf Courses in the United States *83*
6 Tips from the Pros on How to Speed Up Golf Play *84*
Danny Lawler's Top 10 and Second 12 Golf-Playing Baseball Players *84*
Hubert Mizell's 5 Worst Failures for a Golfer *87*

VII THE CITY GAME *89*

Nancy Lieberman's 10 Greatest Professional Basketball Players (Men) of All Time *89*
The 2 Most Smashing Backboard Shootouts *90*
25 Memorable Dates in the History of Basketball *93*
3 Living Members of the Basketball Hall of Fame Who Are Older Than the Sport Itself *94*
The Only 6 Players to Make the All-American High School Basketball Team 3 Times *95*
Mel Greenberg's 15 Major Developments, 12 Greatest Players, and 14 Greatest Coaches in Women's Basketball Over the Past Decade *95*

VIII WHAT'S IN A NAME? *107*

Stan Isaacs' Alphabetical Hall of Fame *107*
20 Beautiful Names from the Ranks of Football *108*
Kevin Demarrais' All-Ivy League Tweedy Name Team *108*
Michael Kunstler's 17 Jurisprudence All-Stars *111*
8 Baseball Players in Major League History with 13 Letters in Their Last Names *113*
13 Sports Personalities Better Known as "Dutch" Than by Their Real First Names *113*
Bill O'Donnell's 10 Favorite Baseball Nicknames *115*
Roy Blount, Jr.'s 15 Major Sports Juniors *115*

IX WINTER WONDERLAND *119*

Hugh Delano's Potpourri of Hockey, from Great Names, Past and Present, to Cigar Smokers, to Best Dressed, to Haircuts, to Meanies, to Intellectuals, to . . . *119*
Art Devlin's 10 Greatest Ski Jumpers *131*
Freestyle America's 10 Greatest Combined Freestyle Skiers of All Time *131*
Bob Perry's 10 Greatest Skiing Photographers *134*
Lou Goldstein's 10 Greatest Barrel Jumpers *134*

X GALLOPING GOURMETS *139*

Tom Lasorda's Ratings of Food in National League Clubhouses *139*
Baseball Players' 10 Favorite Restaurants in New York *141*
Maury Allen's 10 Best and Worst Free-Load Goodies in Baseball Press Boxes *141*
Captain Moss Bunker's 10 Favorite Fish *141*

XI A KICK IN THE GRASS 143

Temple Pouncey's Best Players, Best Americans, Biggest Flops, Nastiest, Sneakiest, Ugliest, Most Inspirational, Most Overrated, Most Underrated, Gunners, Best Shooters, Fastest, Best Goalkeepers, Flakiest, Best and Worst Places to Play, Most Poorly Run Franchises and Cutest Teams in Soccer *143*

Real Names of 13 Well-Known Soccer Players *150*

Jerry Trecker's 7 Greatest Soccer Memories *150*

Barry Janoff's 13 Soccer Players Who Know Their Game *152*

XII BACK IN THE SADDLE 155

Sam "The Genius" Lewin's 10 Greatest Thoroughbreds, Trainers, and Jockeys of All Time *155*

Jim Bolus' 15 Favorite Names of Kentucky Derby Starters, and How They Got Them *156*

Patrick Premo's 18 Thoroughbreds Who Never Lost a Race *163*

XIII MATCH POINT! 165

Lance Tingay's 10 Greatest Matches at Wimbledon *165*

Steve Flink's Top 10 Men and Top 10 Women Tennis Players of the 1970s *166*

Steve Flink's 10 Best Tennis Matches of the 1970s *168*

XIV THE FOURTH ESTATE 169

Bill Gallo's 11 Easiest Sports Faces to Draw *169*

The 10 Most Powerful Baseball Writers in America *169*

34 Writers and Photographers Who Have Covered Every Super Bowl *173*

Bill Libby's 15 Good Guys and 15 Bad Guys in Sports *174*

XV THE MANLY ART *179*

Sylvester Stallone's 5 Favorite Fights *179*

10 Fights Harry Markson Would Have Liked to Promote *179*

Angelo Dundee's 10 Greatest Left-Handed Fighters *180*

XVI SHAPING UP *183*

Walt "Clyde" Frazier's 10 Grooming Secrets *183*

LeRoy Neiman's 5 Sexiest Women in Sports *184*

Jayne Kennedy's 9 Sexiest Men in Sports *184*

Bill Starr's 10 Golden Rules of Rehabilitation for the Injured Athlete *186*

The 8 Greatest Training Rules of the Roaring '90s, as Prescribed by Top Professional Trainer W. W. Morgan, That Stand the Least Chance of Being Adopted in 1980 *186*

Dr. Allan J. Ryan's 4 Medical Sports Myths About the Care and Feeding of Athletes *188*

XVII HALLS OF IVY *191*

Stan and Natalie Isaacs' 12 Most Beautiful College Campuses in the Land *191*

10 Sure Ways for the Athletic Director to Make His Coaches Hate Him *192*

10 Sure Ways for the Coach to Make the Faculty Hate Him *193*

Stan Saplin's One Dozen (Not So Shrinking) Violets from NYU *195*

Hubert Mizell's 10 Most Prestigious College Football Coaching Jobs *195*

Hubert Mizell's 7 Most Prestigious College Basketball Coaching Jobs *195*

Abe Goteiner's Top 10 NAIA School Alumni *196*

George E. Killian's 10 Greatest Former Junior College Basketball Players Who Made the NBA *196*

XVIII BY THE SEA *199*

James "Doc" Counsilman's 10 Greatest Men and 10 Greatest Women Swimmers of All Time *199*

Tom Hetzel's 10 Greatest Men and 10 Greatest Women Channel Swimmers of All Time *200*

Thomas C. Hardman's 10 Firsts and Foremosts of Water Skiing *204*

The 10 Best Beach Volleyball Players and 5 Best Beach Volleyball Teams of All Time *206*

XIX THE CHECKERED FLAG *209*

Bob Cutter's 22 Famous Sons, 1 Daughter, 17 Brother Acts, 1 Half-Brother Act and 2 Brother-Sister Acts in Auto Racing *209*

XX HO-HUM *219*

Blackie Sherrod's 18 Most Overrated Things in American Sports *219*

Ray Fitzgerald's 10 Most Boring Moments in Sports *220*

Jay Simon's 10 Biggest Bores (Living or Dead) in Sports History *220*

XXI A MIXED BAG *221*

Gerald Dumas' 9 Rules of Etiquette for the Well-Mannered Runner *221*

Ron Guidry's 3 Favorite Places to Hunt *223*

Roy Blount's 5 Best Airports *223*

Minnesota Fats' 10 Best Pre-1950 and 10 Best Modern Pool Players *224*

Minnesota Fats' 5 Greatest Celebrity Pool Players *228*
Pat McDonough's 5 Super Southpaws of Bowling *228*
Milt Roth's 10 Greatest Jai-Alai Players Ever to Perform in the United States *230*
Phyllis Hollander's 10 Champion Sports Mothers *233*
Bert Smith's 10 Greatest Cricket Players of All Time *236*
George Gipe's 10 Favorite Sports Oddities *237*
Ginny Akabene's 13 All-Time Women's Squash Champions *239*
10 Points to Keep in Mind When Officiating Sports at Any Level *239*
Satch Furman's 10 Best (or Worst) Promotions *241*
A List of Lists for *The Book of Sports Lists #3* *243*

I

The Way It Was

King Tut's 10 Favorite Sports

From 1976 through 1979, in the most spectacular art show in American history, more than seven million people flocked to museums around the country to view the Treasures of Tutankhamen exhibit. Arnold C. Brackman, author of a trilogy of best-sellers on archaeology—*The Dream of Troy, The Luck of Nineveh,* and *The Search for the Gold of Tutankhamen*—in addition to being the co-author of *The Gold of Tutankhamen,* with a member of Egypt's Supreme Council on Archaeology, last year secretly unearthed the lost Tut Tapes. The tapes were buried with the boy monarch almost 3,500 years ago.

Although he admits he is having trouble with "gaps" in the tapes, Brackman has uncovered sensational historical information on the life and times of King Tut. For example, one tape disclosed that Tut majored in plumbing at Karnak U. "I was a pharaoh faucet major," Tutankhamen said. Tut also revealed that he was a sports enthusiast and that he earned a "K" in varsity sports for pyramid climbing, pyramid sliding, felucca racing on the Nile, and a game known as "batball," which may have been the precursor to American baseball.

These are Tut's 10 favorite sports according to the tapes:

Ray Fitzgerald's 10 Vanishing Americanisms in Sport

As a columnist for the *Boston Globe,* Ray Fitzgerald is never listless.

1. Punting on third down
2. Kids choosing up sides with a bat
3. Black high-cut basketball sneakers
4. Goalies without masks
5. Two woods
6. Western Union operators in press boxes
7. Drop kicks
8. Scoreless ties
9. Square, wooden backboards
10. White tennis balls

Jerry Green's 17 Favorite Professional Teams That No Longer Exist

Jerry Green, who is not extinct, can be found every day in the sports pages of the *Detroit News,* for which he writes a lively, readable column.

1. Detroit Wheels—World Football League
2. Brooklyn Dodgers—National League
3. Montreal Maroons—National Hockey League

The Montreal Maroons are gone, but their goalie, Clint Benedict, left his trademark, hockey's first face mask, worn in the 1929–30 season.

Hockey Hall of Fame

Brooklyn's Ebbets Field—the way it was. *UPI*

4. Providence Steam Rollers—National Basketball Assn.
5. Boston Bees—National League
6. New York Americans—National Hockey League
7. Miami Seahawks—All-America Football Conference
8. Sheboygan Redskins—National Basketball Assn.
9. Boston Yanks—National Football League

10. Boston Redskins—National Football League
11. Boston Patriots—American Football League
12. Los Angeles Dons—All-America Football Conference
13. Portland Storm—World Football League
14. California Golden Seals—National Hockey League
15. Michigan Stags—World Hockey Assn.

16. Chicago Stags—National Basketball Assn.
17. Washington Nationals—American League

NOTE: The Detroit Wheels and the Portland Storm of the WFL, the Miami Seahawks and the Los Angeles Dons of the AAFC, the Michigan Stags of the WHA, and the Boston Patriots of the AFL have the added distinction of being not only teams that no longer exist but in leagues that no longer exist.

10 Obsolete Olympic Events That Would Be Nice to See Again

1. Tug of war
2. Rope climb
3. Indian club swinging
4. Plunge for distance
5. Two-hand discus
6. Two-hand shot put
7. Two-hand javelin
8. Single stick fencing
9. Dueling pistol
10. Game shooting

George Gipe's 20 Favorite Old-Time Major League Baseball Teams with Unusual Nicknames

1. Fort Wayne Kekiongas (National Association, 1871)
2. Elizabeth Resolutes (National Association, 1873)
3. Middletown Mansfields (National Association, 1872)
4. Cleveland Spiders (National League, 1889–99)
5. Boston Beaneaters (National League, 1883–1906)
6. Boston Doves (National League, 1907–08)
7. Boston Pilgrims (National League, 1909–11)
8. Brooklyn Bridegrooms (National League, 1890–98)
9. Chicago Orphans (National League, 1898)
10. Boston Somersets (American League, 1901–04)
11. Boston Puritans (American League, 1905–06)
12. Cleveland Molly McGuires (American League, 1912–14)
13. Chicago Whales (Federal League, 1914–15)
14. St. Louis Terriers (Federal League, 1914–15)
15. Baltimore Terrapins (Federal League, 1914–15)
16. Newark Peppers (Federal League, 1915)
17. Brooklyn Tip-Tops (Federal League, 1914–15)
18. Brooklyn Wonders (Players' League, 1890)
19. Pittsburgh Burghers (Players' League, 1890)
20. Troy Haymakers (National Association, 1871–72)

George Gipe's 10 Favorite Old-Time Professional Football Teams with Unusual Nicknames

1. Columbus Panhandles (National Football League, 1920–22)
2. Evansville Crimson Giants (National Football League, 1921–22)
3. Racine Legion (National Football League, 1922–24, 1926)
4. Duluth Eskimos (National Football League, 1926–27)
5. Orange Tornadoes (National Football League, 1929)
6. Staten Island Stapletons (National Football League, 1930–32)
7. St. Louis Gunners (American Football League, 1934)
8. Columbus Bullies (American Football League, 1940–41)
9. Philadelphia-Pittsburgh Steagles (National Football League, 1943)
10. Jacksonville Sharks (World Football League, 1974)

II

Arts And Leisure

Tom Gunderson's 10 Greatest Roller Coasters

Tom Gunderson, of Port Charlotte, Fla., is a self-admitted "roller coaster fanatic. Whenever I go to an amusement park (I'm also an amusement park fanatic), I head for the roller coasters. As of this writing, no roller coaster has defeated me (where I would never want to go on it again). One of the physical attributes that enables me to do this without fear is an iron stomach. I once downed a heaping bowl of spaghetti seconds before going on one of these. So, here is my list, selected in order of preference."

1. The Mindbender—Six Flags Over Georgia, Atlanta, Ga.
2. The Hurricane—Circus World, 10 minutes from Disney World, Barnum City, Fla.
3. The Runaway Train—Six Flags Over Texas, Dallas-Ft. Worth, Tex.
4. The Screamin' Eagle—Six Flags Over Mid-America, St. Louis, Mo.
5. The Python—The Dark Continent, Busch Gardens, Tampa, Fla.
6. The Great American Scream Machine—Six Flags Over Georgia, Atlanta, Ga.

The Mindbender in Atlanta.

Six Flags over Georgia

7. Willard's Whizzer—Great America, Gurnee, Ill.
8. Space Mountain—Disney World, Orlando, Fla.
9. Turn of the Century—Great America, Gurnee, Ill.
10. Jet Racers—Six Flags Over Texas, Dallas-Ft. Worth, Tex.

Gunderson adds: "It was tough to decide in which order the top three should be, but after that it was fairly easy to decide. Another thought: Don't think the Runaway Train in Six Flags Over Georgia is as good as the one in Texas, because it isn't. If your sole reason for going to Disney World is to ride Space Mountain, don't go. Space Mountain, in my opinion, is a vastly overpublicized, overrated roller coaster."

George Kolombatovich's 10 Greatest Opera Duels

Operas generally have someone getting TB or getting stabbed. The combat choreographer takes care of the latter by seeing to it that the audience doesn't laugh and that the singer's family doesn't cry. George Kolombatovich is head coach of fencing at Columbia University, and as combat choreographer at the Metropolitan Opera he teaches the opera singers how to duel. His 10 greatest opera duels are listed alphabetically.

1. *Andrea Chenier,* by Umberto Giordano—Act II: Chenier wounds Gerard with his court sword. Had to have a sword fight in this opera—Giordano's father was a fencing master.
2. *Carmen,* by Georges Bizet—Act II: Jose fights Zuniga with sabres; no one is hurt as gypsies enter and separate the antagonists. The gypsies end another fight in Act III, between Jose and Escamillo, this time fought with navajas. Gypsies travel all over.
3. *Don Giovanni,* by Wolfgang Amadeus Mozart—Act I: Baritones (or basses) who sing the title role love the chance to win a fight (instead of the usual tenor), as Giovanni does with his rapier in dispatching the *commendatore.* Had to be included in my list in honor of the librettist, Lorenzo de Ponte, who taught at Columbia.
4. *Faust,* by Charles Gounod—Act IV: Faust mortally wounds Valentin with his rapier when Mephistopheles intervenes. Hell of a fight.
5. *Macbeth,* by Giuseppe Verdi—Act IV: Great battle scene (over 70 people fighting on stage in the Met production) that culminates with Macduff cutting Macbeth with his broad-

sword. Macbeth, dying, sings, "*Mal per me* (It's bad for me)," one of opera's great understatements.

6. *Otello,* by Giuseppe Verdi—Act I: Cassio gets drunk, is tricked into drawing his rapier, attacks Montano, wounds Montano, loses his command. Moral: Don't get drunk.
7. *Romeo and Juliet,* by Charles Gounod—Act III: Rapiers and daggers are everywhere as Capulets and Montagues brawl, with Tybalt fighting and killing Mercutio, followed by Romeo fighting and killing Tybalt. A .500 batting average is great in baseball, but Tybalt's .500 average in sword fighting has no future.
8. *Tales of Hoffman,* by Jacques Offenbach—Act II: Hoffman uses a court sword to fight Schlemil. Schlemil dies, but, then, how could anyone named Schlemil win?
9. *Tristan and Isolde,* by Richard Wagner—Act III: Legendary times require broadswords to be used, as Kurvenal kills Melot and is then critically wounded as the battle continues.
10. *Il Trovatore,* by Giuseppe Verdi—Acts I and II: Both acts end with Manrico and the Count di Luna in the middle of a rapier fight—perhaps Verdi didn't like his combat choreographer.

Herman L. Masin's 29 Prize-Winning Book Titles That Were Just Dying for a Designated Writer

Herman L. Masin is editor of *Scholastic Coach* magazine.

1. Thomas Wolfe: *Look Homeward, Angel Cordero*
2. Charles E. Lindbergh: *The Spirit of St. Louis Carnesecca*
3. Barbara W. Tuchman: *The Guns of August Busch*
4. Lillian Hellman: *Watch on the Rhine Duren*
5. Booth Tarkington: *The Magnificent Sparky Ambersons*
6. Thornton Wilder: *The Bridge of San Luis Ray Klivecka*
7. Edward Everett Hale: *The Man Without a Country Slaughter*
8. Arthur Kopit: *Oh Dad, Poor Dad, Mama's Hung You in the Closet and I'm Feeling So Sad Sam Jones*
9. Carson McCullers: *The Heart Is a Lonely Catfish Hunter*
10. Marc Connelly: *The Sihugo Green Pastures*
11. Erma Bombeck: *The Grass Is Always Greener Over the Septic Tank Younger*

12. Ernest Hemingway: *Across the Mickey Rivers and Into the Trees*
13. William Shakespeare: *Enrique Romo and Juliet*
14. Eugene O'Neill: *Anna Christie Mathewson*
15. Robert Sherwood: *There Shall Be No Bobby Night*
16. Neil Simon: *Last of the Red Auerbach Hot Lovers*
17. Damon Runyon: *Ray Guys and Dolls*
18. Clifford Odets: *Waiting for Lefty O'Doul*
19. John Patrick: *Teahouse of the August Wally Moon*
20. Elmer Rice: *Gabby Street Scene*
21. George Kelly: *Roger Craig's Wife*
22. Anne Frank: *The Diary of Anne Frank Gifford*
23. Frank D. Gilroy: *The Subject Was Pete Roses*
24. Tennessee Williams: *Cat Metkovich on a Hot Tin Roof*
25. Arthur Conan Doyle: *The Adventures of Sherlock Larry Holmes*
26. Irwin Shaw: *The Young Ted Lions*
27. Herman Melville: *Moby Dick Williams*
28. Laurence Sterne: *Tristram Shandy Hogan*
29. Saul Bellow: *Steve Henderson: The Rain King*

Harvey Sabinson's 15 Musicals or Plays Rewritten for Bowie Kuhn

Through the years, there have been several legitimate Broadway productions that had to do, in some measure, with sports. Number among them *Damn Yankees* (baseball), *The Changing Room* (British rugby), *Tall Story* and *That Championship Season* (basketball), and *The Great White Hope* (boxing). On the other hand, there have been innumerable plays and musicals that from their titles sounded as if they had to do with sports—but didn't. A Broadway pundit, Harvey Sabinson, who toils for the League of New York Theaters and Producers, has compiled a list of these. Giving rein to his fertile imagination, Sabinson has dreamed up some plots that these shows might have had if they indeed did not belie their titles.

Sabinson, who spent 27 years as a leading theatrical press agent and is the author of "Darling, You Were Wonderful," has some obscure credentials in the universe of sports. He was manager of his college basketball and baseball teams, on which one of the co-authors of this book played in callower days. His Broadway sports list deals only with his favorite sport, baseball.

1. *Look Homeward, Angel*—Chet, a star outfielder for Gene Autry's Anaheim bunch, hits a triple in the first act with none out. He gazes longingly at home plate during the next two acts as the next three batters pop out. In Act III, he dies at third.
2. *The Indian Wants the Bronx*—Bobby, a Cleveland pitcher, demands to be traded to the Yankees. He harangues his general manager until he gets his wish. Then he's sorry.
3. *Red Gloves*—Maggie, a freaked-out leather craftsperson, is starving in Vermont making wallets, until her talents are discovered by a scout for the Cincinnati Reds, who gets her a contract to make gloves for his team.
4. *Tiger at the Gates*—A musical that follows the fortunes of the Detroit Tigers through a tight pennant race that sees them lose on the last day of the season.
5. *The Coach with Six Insides*—Herb, a nervous coach with the Texas Rangers, is troubled by digestive problems. After his sixth operation, his ailment is cured.
6. *Miracle in Brooklyn*—This fantasy conjectures on the return of the Dodgers to their point of origin. A housing project in Brooklyn is torn down by order of Mayor Ed Koch, and a ballpark is erected on the site. It is named Ebbets Field.
7. *St. Louis Woman*—A musical starring Carol Channing as Molly, the first female to make the majors. She is signed by the St. Louis Cardinals as a pitcher, wins 29 games during the regular season, two each in the playoffs and World Series. The big number comes as the Cardinals win the Series. It's called, "Hello, Molly."
8. *The Birds*—A Greek tragedy about Earl, a manager of the Orioles, who smokes himself to death in the dugout.
9. *A Midsummer Night's Dream*—Joe, a general manager of the Mets, dreams that on a night in mid-July, 55,000 fans pack Shea Stadium to see the Mets slaughter the Pirates, 19-0. He wakes up to find it's only a dream.
10. *Cry of Players*—A drama about a team whose manager is fired after he punches every fan seated behind the first-base dugout. The team repairs to the locker room to shed tears.
11. *Two Little Girls in Blue*—A light musical about Cherry and Merry, who become the first female major league umpires. In the process, they learn a lot of four-letter words.
12. *The Autumn Garden*—During the World Series, Buster, a left fielder with the Twins, sees his life pass before him as he awaits a towering fly. He drops it.

13. *Memphis Bound*—Chico, a 15-year veteran, is sent down to the minor leagues. He refuses to report until he is offered Linda, the daughter of the Memphis owner.
14. *Four in a Garden*—Billy, an innovative manager, stations four outfielders in right field in a futile attempt to stop Dave, the league's leading hitter. The outfielders crash into each other.
15. *Triple Play*—Hank, a third baseman, catches a line drive, steps on third, tags a runner, and joins Bill Wambsganss in the record books.

Rocky Balboa (Sylvester Stallone) meets Apollo Creed (Carl Weathers) in

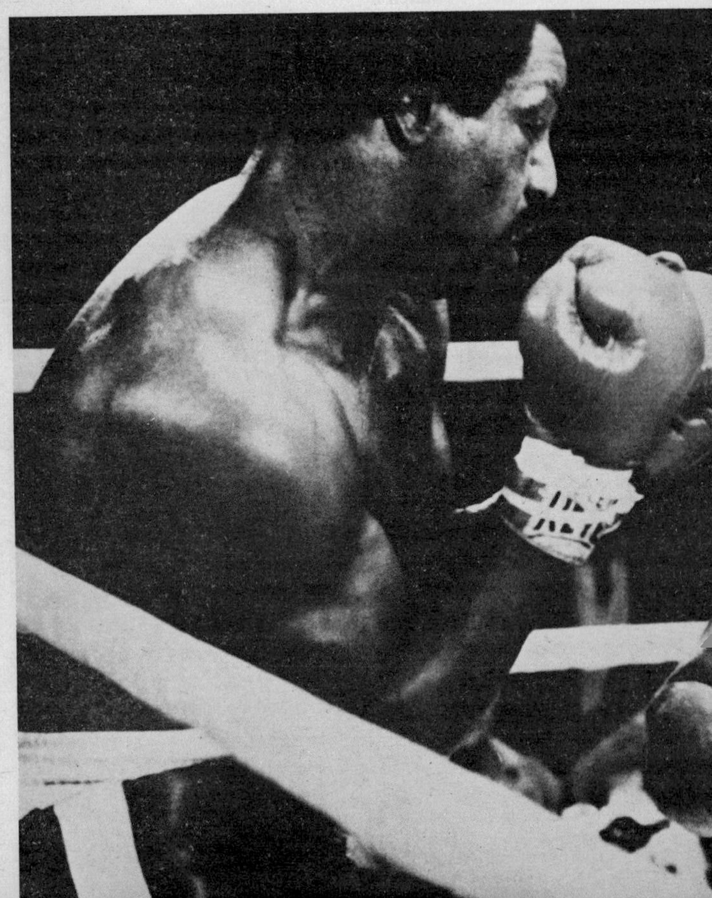

Don Dunphy's 10 Favorite Boxing Movies

Still the best boxing broadcaster in the business, Don Dunphy began his career by broadcasting the Joe Louis—Billy Conn fight in 1941.

1, *The Crowd Roars*—Starring Robert Taylor
2. *Killer McCoy*—Starring Mickey Rooney
3. *Rocky II*
4. *Matilda*—A kangaroo fights for the heavyweight title.
5. *The Ragin' Bull*—The story of Jake LaMotta

the heavyweight title rematch in "Rocky II." *United Artists*

6. *I'll Get By*—The story of Rocky Marciano
7. *The Greatest*—The Muhammad Ali story.
8. *Rocky*
9. *Golden Boy*—The Clifford Odets classic
10. *The Leather Pushers*—By H. C. Witwer, starring Reginald Denny

Dunphy adds: "I had prominent parts in *Matilda, The Greatest, The Raging Bull,* and *I'll Get By,* so perhaps I'm prejudiced."

Paul Newman in "Slap Shot." *Universal*

10 Hollywood Movies with a Hockey Theme

John Wayne and Ronald Reagan on skates? You can look it up. Both these actors appeared in movies with a hockey theme, of which there have been at least 10 in the United States—most of them made in the 1930s, some in the 1970s. Needless to say, there have been many Canadian films with a hockey theme.

1. *Idol of the Crowds,* 1937—Starring John Wayne. Yes, John Wayne plays a hockey player, but a stuntman does the skating scenes.
2. *Hell's Kitchen,* 1939—Ronald Reagan and the Dead End Kids meet the New York Americans.
3. *King of Hockey,* 1939—Starring Wayne Morris.
4. *The Duke of West Point,* 1939—Starring Louis Hayward.
5. *It's a Pleasure,* 1945—Starring Sonja Henie and Michael O'Shea.
6. *Love Story,* 1971—Starring Ryan O'Neal and Ali MacGraw.
7. *Paperback Hero,* 1973—Starring Keir Dullea.
8. *Hockey Homicide,* 1975—A Walt Disney animation in which Goofy plays a goalie.
9. *Slap Shot,* 1977—Starring Paul Newman.
10. *Ice Castles,* 1979—Starring Robby Benson and Lynn-Holly Johnson.

SOURCE: John Halligan, Director of Public Relations and business manager, New York Rangers.

Jack Keane's 12 Greatest Movie Fencers

A creative director for the New York advertising company David, Oksner & Mitchneck, Inc., Jack Keane is a fencer and movie buff in his other life. He was a member of the United States Olympic Team in 1968 and 1972 and captain of the team in 1976 and 1980.

1. Cornell Wilde—"Easily the best fencing actor. He is a trained fencer who fenced at the City College of New York."
2. Basil Rathbone—"A bonafide competitor. One of the few movie people who left a legacy to fencing—money for medals to the Metropolitan Division of the Amateur Fencing League of America."
3. Mel Ferrer—For his swordsmanship in *Scaramouche.*
4. Douglas Fairbanks, Sr.
5. Errol Flynn—A renowned swordsman.
6. Henry Wilcoxen—Son-in-law of Cecil B. DeMille.
7. Rudolph Valentino—Sheik and sabre.
8. Douglas Fairbanks, Jr.
9. Jose Ferrer—Cyrano was his only duel.
10. Stewart Granger
11. David Hemmings—Showed great sabre control in *Far from the Madding Crowd.*
12. Tony Curtis—A fencing enthusiast.

Douglas Fairbanks, Sr., portrayed d'Artagnan in "The Iron Mask."

Joe DiMaggio at 18—in his pre-Yankee days as a San Francisco Seal, with manager Ike Caveney.

UPI

III

Play Ball

Joe DiMaggio's 4 Greatest Highlights of His Career

On the occasion of his 65th birthday—November 25, 1979—Joe DiMaggio agreed to an interview during which he discussed the highlights of his great career. Asked to select his all-time Yankee team and all-time opponent team, DiMaggio declined. "I'd rather not get into that," he said. "I'd leave somebody off who deserves to be on." However, he did agree to choose two players he would pick if he were starting a team from scratch. "My hitter would be Ted Williams," he said. "My pitcher would be Bobby Feller."

1. Playing on 10 American League championship teams and nine World Championship teams in 13 seasons: "That was the most outstanding thing about my career, the highlight, playing with so many world champions; playing with so many great guys through the years. One of my biggest thrills was reporting to spring training in St. Petersburg for the first time in 1936. I had driven from San Francisco with Tony Lazzeri and Frank Crosetti. It took five days. I walked into this dingy clubhouse that had spikes to hang our clothes, and I looked around and there was Bill Dickey, Charley Ruffing, Lou Gehrig, all these great players I had read about, and it was a thrill to meet these fellows."

2. Hitting in 56 consecutive games in 1941: "The Yankees had packed the park day after day because of the streak, everybody anticipating the record. After the season, I went to Ed Barrow (Yankee general manager) and asked for more money. He said it was going to be difficult to give me more because he didn't know where we were going—World War II had just broken out. He offered me a contract with a $5,000 cut. I walked out of his office without signing and went to my apartment on Riverside Drive. When I got there, Mark Roth, our traveling secretary, was waiting for me. He had beat me home, and he was waiting with a contract that called for the same money as the 1941 season, $37,500. That's what got out in the newspapers. There was no mention of the $5,000 they wanted to cut me. It also got out that I was asking for a $5,000 raise, and I got tons of mail denouncing me. 'My boy is in the service making $21 a month and you're asking $42,500.' "
3. Coming back in Boston after missing the first 65 games of the 1949 season because of the removal of a bone spur on his right heel, and hitting four home runs and driving in nine runs in a three-game series: "For four days before the Boston series, I took batting practice in New York, with Gus Niarhos catching and Al Schacht, 60 years old at the time, pitching. Nobody knew when I was going to play. When reporters asked Casey Stengel when I was going to play, Casey said, 'When Joe feels he's ready to come back, I will put him in the lineup.'

   "But I knew when I was going to play. I wasn't going to give that Boston ballpark up. We were only going to play there one more time that year. What better place to come back?

   "On the day of the first game of the Series, I flew up to Boston. I didn't go to the hotel. I went straight to the ballpark, got into my uniform, and went out to the dugout. Stengel was sitting with his back to me, talking to reporters. They were all asking for the starting lineup. 'I can't give you the lineup yet,' Casey said, and he kept looking at me as I was tying my shoe. He kept looking and looking and I never said a word. Finally I nodded my head. And Casey said, 'Now I can give you the lineup.'

   "The first time up, I just couldn't seem to get around on the ball. Mickey McDermott was pitching, and he could throw hard and my timing was off. I kept fouling pitches off to right field, but each time I fouled one off, I got around on the ball a little more. Finally, I hit it over the shortstop's head for a single. The next time up, I hit one out of the park. And that started it. And believe me, what I did in those three games was more surprising to me than anybody else."

4. Winning Game No. 2 of the 1950 World Series with a home run in the 10th inning, off Robin Roberts of the Philadelphia Phillies: "Up to that time, I hadn't had a hit in the Series. The Phillies started Jim Konstanty in the first game, a surprise because he was a relief pitcher. He pitched a great game, but we won, 1-0. But Konstanty held me hitless.

   "When I came to bat in the 10th inning of the second game against Roberts, I was still hitless—nothing for seven or eight in the Series. The score was tied, 1-1. I remember Bugs Baer wrote that I was hitting up a smokestack, and that's what I was doing.

   "Before the game, I asked John Mize what Roberts threw, because he had hit against him in the National League. He said he threw a fastball and a curve. I asked him what his fastball did, and he said it bore in on you. So I tried to open up on him so I wouldn't get jammed, but his fastball kept tailing away from me, not bearing in, and I kept popping him up. I decided to use my own judgment and to concentrate a little harder, and in the 10th inning, I hit one out of the park and we won the game, 2-1."

Joel Stein's 11 Best Letters from Baseball's All-Time Old-Timers

As a young boy, Joel Stein, former advertising man and now a corporate bond broker with Cowen and Co. in New York City, did what boys still do—collect autographs of baseball stars. After a few summers of frequenting the players' entrances at Yankee Stadium and the Polo Grounds and the lobbies of the Commodore and New Yorker hotels, he had accumulated all the autographs he could of the current crop of players, so he decided to seek the autographs of the old-timers of his dad's day—Cobb, Ruth, Gehrig, Sisler, Mathewson, Young, and Wagner. He compiled a list of the names and addresses of old-time players and executives and wrote to them. He asked specific questions to be certain the old-times would respond with more than just an autograph. In two years, he acquired letters, autographs, and photographs of 54 baseball greats. Following are excerpts from the best of those letters, with grammar, punctuation, and capitalization exactly as it appears in the letters.

1. Dear Joel:
   . . . this is haytime. We need rain badly so we will have some feed for cows and horses. I will be up in New York later this month [EDITOR'S NOTE: for a war-bond drive]. I expect they will have a fine time at the Polo Grounds, also take in lots of money which will help end this war.
   Sincerely,
   Walter Johnson
   Germantown, Md.
   August 6, 1943

2. (Response to the question "What do you think about continuing baseball during the war years?")
   Dear Joel Stein:
   . . . I think baseball our national pastime should be carried on for it happens to be apart of our national life, beyond the morale idea it is a fine developer physically for young Americans, no game we play develops a man's initiative as baseball, also baseball is less dangerous, each man defensively has his own territory to protect and outside of some coaching no one can aid him in taking care of all that comes in his field.
   Sincerely,
   Ty Cobb
   Box 394D
   Menlo Park, California
   January 3rd 1944

3. (Response to the question "Who do you consider the all-time third baseman?")
   My dear Mr. Stein:
   . . . I have always felt that its a matter of opinion in regards to who may be the best player—Traynor (Pie) being in the National Leagur did not see him play many games—Collins (Jim) was in the American League—was really a great player. Also here, Traynor as was Collins has been considered the best by Newspaper men.
   Connie Mack
   January 5, 1944

Connie Mack and one of his Athletics, Al Simmons, who had more than 3,000 hits.

UPI

4. Dear Joel:
   . . . I don't consider I was very famous. But Thanks for the compliment. I think Ty Cobb was the greatest all round B.B. player that Ever Lived.
   Yours Very Truly,
   Joe Jackson
   Outfielder
   Greenville, South Carolina
   3-9-44

5. I will make it brief. I am on a farm doing work Just as I can Stand it. feeling fine in good health and ready to go.
   My best to you from
   Cy Young
   Paoli, Ohio
   August 9, 1943

6. (Response to the question "Who was the greatest player of all time?")
   My dear Joel B. Stein
   Babe Ruth was the most sensational as well as the most valuable first because of his powerful home run drives to win games and secondly because of his great drawing power having far surpassed all others, "Honus" Wagner "The Flying Dutchman" was the greatest S.S. of all time and played any and all infield positions in emergencies and being a tremendous hitter was the sensation of his day and the first player to have his photograph's sold at entrances to ball parks. Ty Cobb was the sensation of his day because of his terrific base running ability and also a tremendous and timely hitter.
   Yours truly,
   R. J. Klem
   Chief of Staff
   N.L. Umpires.
   1353 Venetian Way
   Miami, Florida
   March 9, '44

7. My Dear Joel:
   . . . And now beginning my 21st year in the big leagues. I am looking forward to this season with keen anticipation as it will afford me the opportunity to fulfill at least one of my ambitions and that is to be an active player for 20 years in the

Major Leagues (I coached one season). It may also give me a chance to gather up 82 more hits and be the 7th member of that 3000 hit class that includes Cobb, Wagner, Collins, Lajoie, Waner, Speaker and Anson.
Sincerely,
Al Simmons
Phila. Atheletics
1944
Frederick, Maryland
March 24, 1944

8. Dear Mr. Stein:
. . . Anyone who has made a hobby of baseball, whether as a fan, keeping averages of players, or collecting autographs, has always been rewarded with very fine memories in later life.

Connie Mack and Clark Griffith have been in the game more than fifty years and both have been a credit to our great game during their entire connection with baseball. We have had many great players, Ed Delahanty, "Larry" Lajoie, Buck Ewing Charley Bennett, Rube Waddell, Christie Matheson [Matthewson], Hugh Duffy Cy Young Chief Bender, Cap Anson, Jimmy Ryan of the former generation. Babe Ruth, Lou Gehrig, Joe Gordon, George Sisler whom I was sure was going to be the greatest—but whose career was cut short by eye trouble. Urban Shocker a great pitcher who died young, George Mullen, Hank Greenberg of this generation, of course many others whom I cannot recall at this moment. This is just one man's opinion I think Ty Cobb was the greatest all-around player I ever saw, he coud do everything and do them well. Hoping you will live long to enjoy baseball and your autographs.
I remain Sincerely yours,
Bob Quinn
President Boston Braves
Braves Field
March 3, 1944

9. Dear Mr. Stein:
. . . that you also like to have a letter from each of the fellows who are in the Hall of Fame or those who are liable to be in it. Well, I am one of those fellows who is liable to be in as the newspaper boys have been talking about helping me up to

that lofty height. Anyway, I hope I get there for I think it is quite a distinction.
Yours most sincerely,
Clark Griffith
President
Washington Senators
Dec 28, 1943

10. Dear Joel:
. . . I've been very busy with my new duties in Philadelphia [ED. NOTE: general manager of the Phillies]. It looks like a real two-fisted job trying to get the Phillies out of seventh place, but we will give them the best we have and hope to be able to show some improvement. To me, Lou Gehrig was the greatest first baseman of all time. Too bad his career had to end the way it did.
Sincerely yours,
Herb Pennock
January 16, 1944

11. My dear Joel:
Your letter of last month found me very busy. I had a sale at the Ranch and sold off all the livestock and Machinery as help was so scarce that you could not operate [ED. NOTE: World War II was on].
You will note by the letter head that I named the ranch after the Pirate Ball Club and it has quite a reputation in Kansas. It is hard for me to keep up with the new players that come into the game as I have been out of the game since 1915 and that was a long time before you were born.
Very sincerely,
Fred C. Clarke
Little Pirate Ranch
Winfield, Kansas
Feb 10th 1944

Bill Madden's 10 Most Valuable Baseball Cards

Collector and columnist Bill Madden, of the *New York Daily News,* writes a column for *The Sporting News* on his hobby—sports memorabilia.

1. 1910 Piedmont Cigaret (T206) Honus Wagner: About 15 of these are known to exist after Wagner, a non-smoker, in-

WAGNER, PITTSBURG

PLANK, PHILA. AMER.

sisted his card be removed from this set of 523 cards issued by 16 different tobacco companies. Estimated value: $4,500.

2. 1910 Sweet Caporal (T206) Eddie Plank: The Plank card from the same tobacco set is almost as scarce as the Wagner,

due to a printing accident that destroyed its plates. Estimated value: $3,500–$4,000.

3. 1933 Goudey Gum (R319) Napoleon Lajoie: This card, No. 106 in the 1933 Goudey set of 240, was, for some reason, omitted from the original set and was issued in limited quantity in the following year's set. About 15–20 are known to exist. Estimated value: $3,500–$4,000.
4. 1952 Topps Gum (R414-6) Mickey Mantle: While this card is not nearly as scarce as the Wagner, Plank, Lajoie, or even others on this list, it has attained "inflated" value in today's collector's markets because of the preeminence of both Topps and Mantle cards in the modern market. The 1952 Topps set is fairly common except for the last series, 311–410, which was issued late in the year and only in the Northeast. Of those high numbers, the Mantle card, No. 311, has become the most sought by collectors and has risen in value from $25 (the going price for most of the other Topps '52 high numbers) to $2,000 and up.

5. 6. 7. 1951 Topps "Current All Stars," Robin Roberts, Eddie Stanky, and Jim Konstanty: The "Current All-Stars," along with a sister set, "Connie Mack's All-Stars," were 11-card sets that were issued in 1951 as premiums (one to a pack) along with Topps' regular set of cards. These premium cards were a sort of "stiffener" to the pack, since the regular Topps cards that year were folded in the middle. Both "All-Star" sets are worth considerably more than the regular Topps cards they were sold with that year, simply because they were so much scarcer (only one to a pack). The "Modern All-Stars" are worth more than the "Connie Mack All-Stars" because of the greater demand for modern-day players—and of the Modern All-Stars, Stanky, Roberts, and Konstanty appear to be the most rare. Estimated value: $1,500 apiece.

8. 1911 Cigaret Companies (T207) Grover Loudermilk: This was the Cigaret Companies' follow-up set to the most popular T206 set of the year before. The Loudermilk card, for reasons never uncovered, has become the rarest card in this set—probably simply because there were fewer printed. Estimated value: $1,000.
9. 1910 Cigaret Companies (T206) Sherry "Magie": Again, the famous and popular T206 set makes the top 10, this time for its most noted error. Almost every year since cards have been manufactured, there have been error cards in which the

identity of the player, his team, or some other item is misprinted. This was one of the first. Evidently, it was corrected since there are Sherry Magee cards in the T206 set. It's the Sherry Magie—the error card—that is regarded as scarce by the collectors. Both have the same picture, just the name underneath has been changed. Estimated value: $650.

10. 1948 Leaf Gum Satchel Paige: The distribution of this skip-numbered set of cards, issued by the Leaf Gum Co. of Chicago, was severely curtailed by a legal battle between Leaf and the other prominent gum company of the era, Bowman. As a result, the second series in this 98-card set is extremely scarce. The Paige card, No. 8, is considered to be the rarest of all in that series, probably because Paige is a Hall of Famer and 1948 was his best season in a brief major league career. Estimated value: $350–$450. It should be noted that all the cards in that second series are probably as rare as the T206 Wagner card, but they never acquired the same mystique.

Dr. Frances A. Bock's 54 Tobacco Chewers and Their Idiosyncrasies

Dr. Frances A. Bock is a New York psychologist whose interests stretch beyond the traditional limits of her field. They include, for example, sports—probably because her husband, Hal, is baseball editor for the Associated Press. Dr. Bock recently completed a study of tobacco chewing by ball players and the relationship between the handedness (left or right) of the chewers and the side on which they prefer to chew. She found statistical significance in the fact that twice as many right-handed players chew on the left side as chew on the right, while equal numbers of left-handers chew on each side. The preference is apparently related to brain organization, which differs between left-handed people and right-handers.

20 RIGHT-HANDED PLAYERS WHO CHEW TOBACCO ON THE LEFT SIDE

1. Dick Tidrow
2. Catfish Hunter
3. Doug Flynn
4. Tim Foli
5. John Stearns
6. Craig Swan
7. Gene Tenace
8. Rod Carew
9. Glenn Adams
10. Rick Wise
11. Jim Kern
12. Buddy Bell

13. Steve Ontiveros
14. Dan Spillner
15. Frank LaCorte
16. Rick Matula
17. Leon Roberts
18. Billy Smith
19. Skip Lockwood
20. Glenn Abbott

10 RIGHT-HANDED PLAYERS WHO CHEW TOBACCO ON THE RIGHT SIDE

1. Brian Doyle
2. Phil Garner
3. John D'Acquisto
4. Rollie Fingers
5. Dennis Martinez
6. Joe Kerrigan
7. Mike Krukow
8. John Ellis
9. Ferguson Jenkins
10. Gene Garber

8 LEFT-HANDED PLAYERS WHO CHEW TOBACCO ON THE LEFT SIDE

1. Sparky Lyle
2. Rick Honeycutt
3. Ruppert Jones
4. Bruce Bochte
5. Bob Shirley
6. Terry Forster
7. Terry Crowley
8. Tippy Martinez

7 LEFT-HANDED PLAYERS WHO CHEW TOBACCO ON THE RIGHT SIDE

1. Ron Guidry
2. Randy Jones
3. Bob Owchinko
4. Rick Waits
5. Dave Roberts
6. Jon Matlack
7. Mike Lum

8 PLAYERS WHO ARE UNDECIDED AND CHEW ON BOTH SIDES

1. Mario Mendoza
2. Tom Griffin
3. Jim Anderson
4. Ken Landreaux
5. Bobby Valentine
6. Rob Wilfong
7. Butch Wynegar
8. Don Hood

1 PLAYER WHO CHEWS IN THE MIDDLE

1. Bobby Murcer

Moss Klein's 11 Most Memorable (Publicized?) Yankee Controversies, 1977–79

Moss Klein covers the Yankees and their controversies for the *Newark Star-Ledger,* and believes, as do his colleagues, that after three years on the beat, he qualifies for combat pay.

1. The Re-Firing of Billy Martin, October 28, 1979
This came about when Martin, given a second chance to manage the Yankees and warned that he must be on his best behavior, allegedly punched out a Lincolnshire, Ill., marshmallow salesman in the lobby of L'Hotel de France, in Bloomington, Minn. Martin argued that he was acting in self-defense, but Yankee owner George M. Steinbrenner considered it the final straw and replaced Martin with Dick Howser as Yankee manager.
2. The Old-Timers Day Re-Hiring of Billy Martin, July 29, 1978
This was probably the most shocking of all the Martin-Steinbrenner episodes, coming five days after Martin's resignation in Kansas City (see Controversy No. 4) and catching nearly everybody by surprise. This time, Martin was "re-hired" for the 1980 season, and that, of course, led to further controversies and, eventually, to Controversy No. 1.
3. The Billy Martin-Reggie Jackson Dugout Scene, June 18, 1977
This happened on a Saturday afternoon in Boston's Fenway park, in full view of a national television audience and is the highlight of all the Jackson-Martin confrontations. Martin felt that Reggie had loafed on a hit to right field by Jim Rice in the sixth inning, and sent Paul Blair out to replace Jackson in the middle of the inning. As Reggie returned to the dugout, he and Martin were shouting at each other, and the manager was restrained by coaches Yogi Berra and Elston Howard from attacking Jackson.
4. Martin's Resignation, July 24, 1978
After all the near-firings and rumored firings, Martin finally made his tearful resignation in a hotel lobby in Kansas City. The night before, while the Yankees waited in Chicago's O'Hare Airport for the flight to Kansas City, Martin had made his fateful statement, referring to Steinbrenner and Jackson: "The two of them deserve each other," he said. "One's a born liar, the other's convicted." Presumably, Martin was then forced into resigning.
5. The Reggie Jackson Bunting Incident, July 17, 1978
Here's where the stage was set for Controversies No. 2 and No. 4. Jackson, batting in the 10th inning against the Royals at Yankee Stadium, continued to attempt a bunt even though Martin had given the "hit" sign. Reggie eventually struck out, then carefully removed his glasses as he returned to the dugout. But Martin didn't want another scene, so he told coach Gene Michael to inform Reggie that he should leave. A

five-day suspension followed, and then the other controversies developed.

6. Martin Returns as Manager, Bob Lemon Fired, June 18, 1979
News of this actually leaked out two days earlier, but Steinbrenner, attempting to shake the Yankees out of their season-long slump, didn't make any decision until he had met with Martin in Columbus on June 17. Until this move, there had been continuing doubts as to whether Steinbrenner would really bring Martin back for the 1980 season. So he fooled everybody and brought him back sooner.
7. The Rich Gossage-Cliff Johnson Shower Room Fight, April 19, 1979
Proving that the Yankees could have a controversy without Billy, Reggie, or George, the outstanding relief pitcher and the unhappy reserve catcher engaged in their early-season fight that resulted in thumb surgery for Gossage and his absence for more than 12 weeks. The bullpen collapsed without Gossage, the Yankees fell out of the race, the Lemon-Martin maneuver was performed, and Johnson was traded to the Indians.
8. Martin's Fight in Reno with Sportswriter Ray Hagar, Nov. 1978
This led to the continuing doubts that Steinbrenner would bring Martin back. The fight, in which Martin punched Hagar in the face at a basketball game, became a major topic until a settlement was finally reached in late May, 1979.
9. Reggie's No-Handshake Home Run, May 23, 1977
Jackson hit his homer in the seventh inning against the Red Sox, and, instead of heading to the dugout for the customary handshakes, he went directly to the far end of the dugout, avoiding the players and Martin. This was shortly after the *Sport* magazine article in which Reggie had referred to himself as "the straw that stirs the drink" and had belittled Thurman Munson. The incident intensified the already existing tense conditions.
10. The Reggie-Billy World Series Insult, Oct. 13, 1977
Martin had benched Jackson against Royals' lefty Paul Splittorff in the fifth game of the playoffs and Reggie had then become critical of Martin on this off-day before the

This, of course, was before Billy Martin and Reggie Jackson had their 1977 dugout set-to.

UPI

third game of the Series against the Dodgers. "I know what I can do," Reggie said. "If he did, we might be a lot better off." Naturally, Martin didn't like being second-guessed. He made some references to Jackson, concluding with, "If he doesn't like it, he can kiss my dago ass." Reggie went on to set his home-run record as the Yankees won the Series in six games.

11. This spot is reserved for the countless other controversies of the three-year period, far too many to detail. You could choose, for example, from a list including the $2,500 fine levied on Martin by team president Gabe Paul in 1977, or Graig Nettles leaving spring training in a contract dispute in 1977, or any of the Sparky Lyle or Mickey Rivers situations, or Thurman Munson's beard-growing in August, 1977, or the marijuana growing on Don Gullett's farm in 1977, or Al Rosen's resignation as president in July, 1979, or the girl mooning on the bus in August, 1979, or . . .

Furman Bisher's 10 All-Time Baseball Holdouts (Rated on Degree of Stubbornness)

Never a holdout in his career, Furman Bisher is sports columnist and sports editor of the *Atlanta Journal.*

1. Edd Roush: He held out three times, once for an entire season, and still made it to the Hall of Fame.
2. Turkey Mike Donlin: He held out two years in a row, a career record, but spent the time on stage with his wife, Mabel Hite. Otherwise, he would have made it to the Hall of Fame, for he had a lifetime batting average of .333.
3. Frank "Home Run" Baker: He wrote Connie Mack that he should have his contract renegotiated or forget it, which Mr. Mack promptly did. They both made it to the Hall of Fame.
4. Johnny Kling: Held out and ran a pool room in Kansas City for a whole season. Proving he was right all along, the Cubs won the pennant before his holdout and won again the year he returned, but they did not win while Kling was running his pool room.
5. Heinie Groh: Held out in mid-season until Cincinnati sold him to the Giants, whereupon Commissioner Kenesaw Mountain Landis cancelled the deal. Poor Heinie, instead of being with a pennant contender, went back to Cincinnati and the second division.

Babe Ruth comes to terms with Yankee owner Jake Ruppert at the Ruppert Brewery in New York.

UPI

6. Babe Ruth: Held out until Yankee owner Jake Ruppert agreed to pay him $80,000, which was more than President Herbert Hoover was making. "Hell," cracked the Babe, "I had a better year."
7. Sandy Koufax-Don Drysdale: They win the prize for "team" holdout, each agreeing not to sign with the Dodgers until both were satisfied. As a result, both became $100,000 pitchers.
8. Rufe Gentry: Rocked away the summer of 1945 on his front porch, then when the varsity players came home from the war, he found he had no job.

GEM

9. Cliff Bolton: I doubt if he ever really held out. I don't think he ever opened his mail until it was blackberry weather.
10. Bobo Newsom: Always held out just for exercise. He hated spring training.

Red Foley's 10 Baseball Records That Will Never Be Broken

A genuine historian on the grand, old game, Red Foley regularly wrote a column, "Ask Red," for the *New York Daily News,* in which he answered baseball questions from fans.

1. Lou Gehrig's 2,130 consecutive-game streak
2. Johnny Vander Meer's two straight no-hit games
3. Cy Young's 511 career major league victories
4. Connie Mack's 50 years managing the same club
5. Rogers Hornsby's composite five-year batting average of .402 (1921–25)
6. Consecutive .400 seasons, Ty Cobb (1911–12) and Rogers Hornsby (1924–25)
7. Joe DiMaggio's 56-game hitting streak
8. Jack Chesbro's 41 pitching victories in 1904
9. Most consecutive innings pitched without relief: John W. Taylor, Chicago Cubs and St. Louis Cardinals, 203 games, June 20, 1901 through August 9, 1906.
10. Bill Dahlens's career record of 972 errors at shortstop over 20 years, covering 2,139 games

Foley adds: "Two consecutive no-hitters, not an impossibility, would only equal Vander Meer's record. To break his record, a pitcher must pitch three consecutive no-hitters; Dahlen averaged 48.6 errors a season but because of better equipment (gloves), fielders don't miss as many balls, and these days a player would be replaced if he even got close to Dahlen's record."

Lou Gehrig Day at Yankee Stadium—July 4, 1939, when everybody, including Lou, shed a tear.

UPI

Billy Martin's 2 Commandments on How to Keep the Boss Happy

This code, or commandments, hung on the wall of the office of the twice-deposed New York Yankee manager. He says it was given to him by the boss, George Steinbrenner. Martin says it applies not only to Steinbrenner vis-à-vis Martin, but to Martin vis-à-vis his players.

1. The boss is always right.
2. If the boss is wrong, see No. 1.

The irrepressible Pete Rose. *Rich Pilling*

6 Active Baseball Players Who Are Locks for the Hall of Fame

1. Rod Carew
2. Pete Rose
3. Tom Seaver
4. Johnny Bench
5. Carl Yastrzemski
6. Jim Palmer

Selected by Hubert Mizell of the *St. Petersburg* (Fla.) *Times.*

14 Reference Books Without Which a Baseball Library Would Be Incomplete

1. *Baseball Register*—Published annually by *The Sporting News.* Year-by-year records of all the active players on the spring training rosters, and the coaches and managers.
2. *Baseball Guide*—Published annually by *The Sporting News.* Complete statistical and historical review of the preceding season for the major and minor leagues.
3. *Dope Book*—Published annually by *The Sporting News.* Complete records of all All-Star Games and Championship Series games; current rosters, stadium diagrams, and yearly finishes and attendances.
4. *Baseball Record Book*—Published annually by *The Sporting News.* All-time leaders; club and all-time records for regular season play.
5. *World Series Record Book*—Published annually by *The Sporting News.* Complete history of the World Series, including all box scores and records.
6. *The Book of Baseball Records*—Published by Elias Sports Bureau. Rosters of all pennant-winning teams; regular season, World Series, and championship records.
7. *The Baseball Encyclopedia*—Published by Macmillan. Updated periodically. Year-by-year records of all major leaguers in history. The 1969 edition includes pitchers' batting records and year-by-year records for World Series play. Rosters, listings, and more.
8. *The Official Encyclopedia of Baseball*—Published by A. S. Barnes & Co. Paperback edition by Doubleday. Updated frequently. Only source for finding all-time list of umpires.
9. *American League Red Book*—Published annually by MG Book Graphics. Current rosters, team directories, previous season statistics, all-time listings, lifetime records, features.
10. *National League Green Book*—Published annually by MG Book Graphics. Same as *Red Book,* but covering the National League.
11. *Baseball Blue Book*—Published annually by Baseball Blue Book Co. Major league rules and directories of all professional teams. Addresses of managers, coaches, and scouts.
12. Media Guides—Published annually by all teams. Not all on sale to the public. Playing records of all active members of team; historical information, more.
13. *Official Baseball Rules*—Published annually by *The Sporting News.* There are always minor changes each season.

14. *Who's Who In Baseball*—Published annually by Who's Who in Baseball Magazine Co. Year-by-year records of all active players.

SOURCE: Marty Appel, Associate Director of Information, Media, Office of the Baseball Commissioner.

Mel Allen's All-Time Team

For a quarter of a century, from 1939 through 1964, Mel Allen was the "Voice of the Yankees" and the most well-known baseball broadcaster of his time. "Picking an all-star team from among the players I've seen is difficult," he says. "There are so many great players and the distinctions so microscopic that I'm bound to overlook somebody unintentionally. I'm trying to pick my team for balance rather than a bunch of individual stars."

1b. Hank Greenberg
2b. Jackie Robinson
SS. Marty Marion
3b. Red Rolfe
C. Bill Dickey

OF. Ted Williams
Joe DiMaggio
Stan Musial
Mickey Mantle
Willie Mays
Hank Aaron

P. Bob Feller
Carl Hubbell
Whitey Ford
Sandy Koufax

Utility—Tommy Henrich
Manager—Casey Stengel

Adds Allen: "Back of the plate in my time I saw Bill Dickey, and I'd have to rate him No. 1. He taught Berra to catch. I didn't see Mickey Cochrane play, but I did see Gabby Hartnett and Ernie Lombardi. On Lombardi's behalf, I will say that I've talked to many ballplayers and heard them say Lombardi had to be one of the greatest hitters who ever lived, but he was so slow that the infield would play him literally in the outfield and take away many of his hits.

"My first year was Lou Gehrig's last, so I didn't see much of him, and in all honesty can't put him at first base.

"At second, I saw more of Joe Gordon, but Jackie Robinson was such a vital spark for the Dodgers.

"I like Marty Marion at shortstop. He was big and tall—sort of like DiMaggio in center. He'd take one long stride so effortlessly. He'd make a tough catch look easy. He could take one stride where

Jackie Robinson joined the Brooklyn Dodgers, out of Montreal, in 1947.
UPI

a fellow like Phil Rizzuto would take four. Phil had one great year, but having one great year doesn't necessarily make you an all-time player. Then there's Frank Crosetti. He had every trick in the trade down, and had such a brilliant baseball mind.

"I put Red Rolfe at third. Billy Cox was great with the Dodgers for a while, but not for as long as Rolfe. Eddie Mathews was a great home-run hitter, and not a bad fielder, but he wasn't as steady as Rolfe.

"The outfield is where I get into trouble. So much trouble, that I'm going with two outfields."

SOURCE: *Popular Sports Baseball*

The 10 Worst Teams in Baseball History

1. Philadelphia A's, 1916—The 1916 season was unique in American League history. Six clubs finished at .500 and above, and the seventh-place Washington Senators came home with a respectable .497 percentage. Front-running Boston and the six other successful clubs were able to manage such evenly balanced records because of the performance of Connie Mack's atrocious A's, 36–117, 40 games out of first place. A year earlier, Mack had dismantled a championship team, although he retained pitcher Bullet Joe Bush, who won 15 of his team's 36 games, eight by shutout. Elmer Myles won 13. Johnny Nabors started the season with a victory, then dropped 19 in a row. Tom Sheehan was 1–16, Jing Johnson 1–10. Shortstop Whitey Witt made 78 errors; third baseman Charlie Peck kicked in with 42 more.
2. Boston Beaneaters, 1906—This team had four 20-game losers: Irv Young, Gus Dorner, Vive Lindaman, and Jeff Pfeffer. A 19-game losing streak "helped" the Beanies finish 66½ games behind the pennant-winning Cubs, the largest margin in baseball history.
3. Boston Braves, 1935—Wally Berger led the National League with 34 homers and 130 RBI, and a teammate was Babe Ruth (age 40 and winding down his career), but the Braves still finished with a record of 38–115, 61½ games out of first place.
4. New York Mets, 1962—The Amazin' Mets of Casey Stengel were easily the most laughable, most-scoffed-at team in baseball history, winning 40 games and losing 120 in the first year of their existence. They had losing streaks of 13 and 17 games, and once scored 18 runs in a game, prompting one beleaguered Met fan to inquire: "Did they win?"
5. Pittsburgh Pirates, 1952—Catcher Joe Garagiola described this as "the ninth year of (GM) Branch Rickey's five-year

plan." The Pirates finished 42–112, 54½ games out of first, despite the presence of Hall of Famer Ralph Kiner, who belted 37 homers. The Bucs used 16 men in their starting rotation, and the staff walked 615 batters and struck out only 564.

6. St. Louis Browns, 1939—Jack Kramer and Vern Kennedy led the staff with nine victories each for a team that finished 43–111, a record 64½ games behind the leader.
7. Philadelphia A's, 1919—With a pitching staff that had a combined ERA of 4.26 and had posted just one shutout, the A's had a 36–104 record, 52 games out of first.
8. Philadelphia Phillies, 1942—The best hitter for this team of castoffs, has-beens, and never-weres was Danny Litwhiler, who posted mediocre stats of .271, nine homers, and 56 RBI in "leading" the Phillies to a 42–109 finish, 62½ games behind the pace-setting Cardinals.
9. Philadelphia Phillies, 1961—Hall of Famer Robin Roberts entered the 1961 season with 233 career victories and finished the season with 234. This was the nucleus of a potential National League power, but it suffered from growing pains, including a record 23-game losing streak under rookie manager Gene Mauch. The Phillies finished with a record of 47–107, 46 games off the lead.
10. St. Louis Cardinals, 1908—Pitching, they say, is 75 percent of baseball. Not in the case of this team, which had a staff ERA of 2.64. Still, the Cards ended with a record of 49–105, 50 games out of first, because they could not hit. Three regulars batted under .200, and the Cards were shut out 33 times during the season, or once in every five games.

SOURCE: *Baseball* magazine.

IV

First and Ten

Buddy Young's 26 Fastest Backs and 1 Fastest Defensive Lineman of All Time

Claude "Buddy" Young was an 18-year-old freshman at the University of Illinois in 1944 and wouldn't have been playing varsity football had it not been wartime. He was a 5-4½, 165-pound, 9.4 sprinter who proved that a track man could be a football player. In his freshman year, he tied Red Grange's Illini scoring record of 13 touchdowns in a season. After the war, he led Illinois to victory over UCLA in the Rose Bowl, the first one ever played by a Big Ten team.

As a pro, he was the fastest and most spectacular player in the All-America Conference (New York Yankees, 1947–49), and he was a breakaway star for a half-dozen years in the NFL (New York Yanks, Dallas Texans, Baltimore Colts). Today, he is a Director of Player Relations for the NFL.

"I have listed three different categories dealing with speed," Buddy explains. "The first is the start—players moving fastest on the count as the ball is centered. The second is backs who have the ability and speed to get to the hole at the moment it opens. The third is open-field speed, which needs no explanation."

Buddy disqualified himself from contention, but he would make it on anybody else's list.

Sprinter Buddy Young as a broad-jumper at Illinois and as a New York Yankee backfield star.

Buddy Young Collection

6 FASTEST AS THE BALL IS CENTERED

1. Chet Mutryn—Buffalo Bisons, Buffalo Bills, Baltimore Colts
2. Joe Perry—San Francisco 49ers, Baltimore Colts
3. Bobby Mitchell—Cleveland Browns, Washington Redskins
4. Glenn Davis—Los Angeles Rams
5. Marion Motley—Cleveland Browns, Pittsburgh Steelers
6. Billy Vessels—Baltimore Colts, Edmonton Eskimos

10 QUICKEST TO THE HOLE

1. Chet Mutryn—Buffalo Bisons, Buffalo Bills, Baltimore Colts
2. Joe Perry—San Francisco 49ers, Baltimore Colts
3. (tie) Bobby Mitchell—Cleveland Browns, Washington Redskins; Doak Walker—Detroit Lions
5. Lenny Moore—Baltimore Colts
6. Jim Brown—Cleveland Browns
7. Marion Motley—Cleveland Browns, Pittsburgh Steelers
8. Bob "Hunchy" Hoernschmeyer—Chicago Rockets, Brooklyn Dodgers, Chicago Hornets, Detroit Lions

9. Clyde "Smackover" Scott—University of Arkansas, Navy (never played pro ball)
10. Spec Sanders—New York Yankees

Young notes: "I called it a tie for third because if you're talking about from end to end, or straight ahead, Mitchell gets the nod. From tackle to tackle, it's Walker."

11 OPEN-FIELD SWIFTEST

1. Bob Boyd—Los Angeles Rams
2. Bob Hayes—Dallas Cowboys, San Francisco 49ers
3. Elmore Harris—Brooklyn Dodgers
4. Ollie Matson—Chicago Cardinals, Los Angeles Rams, Detroit Lions, Philadelphia Eagles
5. Bobby Mitchell—Cleveland Browns, Washington Redskins
6. Abe Woodson—San Francisco 49ers, Baltimore Colts
7. Dean Renfro—Cleveland Browns
8. Ray Renfro—Cleveland Browns
9. Joe Perry—San Francisco 49ers, Baltimore Colts
10. Spec Sanders—New York Yankees
11. Bill Willis—Cleveland Browns

Young notes: "Willis is the only defensive lineman I picked, and he belongs. Maybe I'm a bit prejudiced. Like me, he was a college sprinter. He came out of Ohio State."

The 6 Commandments of the Church of Monday Night Football

A new religious group was recently organized in Santa Barbara, Calif. Known as The Church of Monday Night Football, it meets every Monday night during the NFL season, in front of a television set. The congregation consists of 600 men and women, under the leadership of its founders, Don Weiner and the Rev. Ricky Slade, an ordained minister in the Universal Life Church.

1. Thou shalt keep Monday night holy . . . and tune in early.
2. Honor thy holy point spread . . . for it is right on.
3. Thou shalt not covet thy neighbor's beer.
4. Thou shalt not commit adultery during halftime highlights.
5. Thou shalt stay tuned until the final gun . . . for the spread may change.
6. Forgive those who bet against their home team . . . for they know not what they do.

> The Commandment After: Prepare for the day when the Super Bowl is played on *Monday Night Football* . . . for on that day there will be heaven on Earth.

Adds Weiner: "We don't want to offend anyone, nor do we want to be sacrilegious. We just want to help people fully enjoy football and have a good time." Weiner also says one of the goals of the group is for Rev. Slade to perform a wedding ceremony during halftime of a Monday night game. Of course, that would cause those attending the wedding to miss the halftime highlights.

Dave Jennings' 11 Biggest Kicking Plays in the NFL Over the Last 25 Years

A six-year veteran of the NFL, New York Giant Dave Jennings has been called "the thinking man's kicker." His letters to the league office were influential in getting the NFL to arrive at a reevaluation of individual statistical standings for punters. Bright and articulate, Jennings is a graduate of St. Lawrence University (his dad is a professor at Southern Connecticut), and he does radio work during the off season. His list, he says, is in chronological order, "with the exception of the two longest kicks, which I have listed last." He modestly omitted his own 58-yard punt against the Buffalo Bills in the final game of the 1974 pre-season which earned him a spot on the Giants. Adds Jennings: "My special thanks to Joe Browne and Susan McCann of the NFL for assisting me in the gathering and compiling of this information with respect to specific teams, dates, names, scores, and other vital statistics."

1. December 14, 1958, Yankee Stadium—The Cleveland Browns vs. the New York Giants in the season finale. Cleveland, with a record of 9–2, led the Eastern Conference ahead of the Giants, 8–3. A victory by the Browns put them in the NFL Championship game with Baltimore; a victory by the Giants would force a one-game playoff between these same two teams the following week. With seconds to go in the game, and the score tied, 10–10, the Giants had the ball "around" the Cleveland 45-yard line. Because of all the snow that had accumulated, the field markings could not be seen. The Giants sent in placekicker Pat Summerall to attempt a field goal of "somewhere between 49 and 56 yards." In the snow, wind, and freezing cold, Summerall put it through the uprights with about 10 yards to spare. Officially, it was a

49-yard field goal, which gave the Giants a 13–10 victory. The Giants then defeated the Browns for the second straight Sunday and proceeded to the championship game.

2. December 28, 1958, Yankee Stadium—In what has been called "the greatest game ever played," the Baltimore Colts and the New York Giants played for the 1958 NFL championship. With the Giants ahead, 17–14, Baltimore's Steve Myhra sent the game into overtime as he hit a 20-yard field goal with seven seconds left in regulation time. The Colts won in overtime, 23–17.
3. December 26, 1960, Philadelphia—The Philadelphia Eagles and the Green Bay Packers met for the 1960 NFL championship at Franklin Field. The Packers led, 13–10, late in the fourth quarter. On the kickoff following Green Bay's go-ahead touchdown, Philadelphia's Ted Dean returned it 58 yards, setting up the winning touchdown. The Eagles won, 17–13.
4. December 26, 1965, Green Bay—The end of the 1965 NFL regular season found Baltimore and Green Bay tied with 10–3–1 records, forcing a playoff game to determine which would meet Cleveland for the league title. The game went into overtime, tied, 10–10. After 13:39 of the overtime, Green Bay's Don Chandler, who had forced the overtime with a 22-yard field goal with 1:58 left in regulation time, hit on a controversial 25-yard field goal to give the Packers a 13–10 victory. The reason for the controversy: The ball was kicked directly above the uprights—it didn't pass through the uprights—and no one could tell for certain if it was good or not. In fact, Chandler's actions immediately after the kick indicated he thought it was no good. As a result of this kick, the uprights were raised the following season to their present height.
5. December 9, 1967, Los Angeles—With two games left in the 1967 season, the Coastal Division of the Western Conference was a tight race. Baltimore was leading at 10–0–2, Los Angeles second at 9–1–2. The Rams, who would meet the Colts in Los Angeles on the last Sunday of the season, had to beat Green Bay to keep pace with Baltimore, which would beat New Orleans that same Sunday. With less than a minute to play in the game, Green Bay, leading 24–20, was forced to

Colts' Jim O'Brien, with Earl Morrall holding, makes the winning kick in Super Bowl V.

UPI

80

punt. The Rams' only hope was to block Donny Anderson's punt and score a quick touchdown. With 54 seconds left, Los Angeles' Anthony Guillory blocked the punt, and Claude Crabb returned it 20 yards to the Green Bay five-yard line. Two plays later, the Rams scored to win, 27–24. The next week, Los Angeles beat Baltimore, 34–10, to win the Coastal Division and go into the conference playoffs.

6. January 17, 1971, Miami—In an error-filled Super Bowl V, rookie place-kicker Jim O'Brien kicked a 32-yard field goal with five seconds left to break a 13–13 tie and give the Baltimore Colts a 16–13 victory over the Dallas Cowboys.
7. December 25, 1971, Kansas City—In a 1967 AFC divisional playoff between Miami and Kansas City, the Dolphins' Garo Yepremian ended the longest game ever—82 minutes, 40 seconds—with a 37-yard field goal, after seven minutes and 40 seconds of the second overtime, to lead Miami to a 27–24 victory over the Chiefs.
8. December 31, 1972, Pittsburgh—The 1972 AFC Championship game between the Miami Dolphins and the Steelers was played at Pittsburgh's Three Rivers Stadium. In the second quarter, with Pittsburgh leading, 7–0, Miami was forced to punt. Dolphin punter Larry Seiple faked the punt and ran 37 yards to set up Miami's first touchdown. The fake turned the game around, helping Miami to a 21–17 victory and enabling the Dolphins to continue in their successful quest of an undefeated season.
9. January 18, 1976, Miami—In the fourth quarter of Super Bowl X, with Dallas leading Pittsburgh, 10–7, the Steelers forced Dallas to punt out of their own end zone. The Steelers' Reggie Harrison broke through to block Mitch Hoopes' punt out of the end zone for a safety. This turned the game around as Pittsburgh went on to score 12 more points after the safety to win, 21–17.
10. September 21, 1969, Denver—The Jets' Steve O'Neil set the standard for punters at Denver's Mile High Stadium. Kicking from the Jet one, his punt rolled dead on the Bronco one, a punt of 98 yards.
11. November 8, 1970, New Orleans—The Saints' Tom Dempsey beat the Detroit Lions with a late field goal that measured 63 yards, the longest ever.

Tom Dempsey, with his sawed-off cleat, kicks his record-breaking 63-yarder.

UPI

19

15-Parilli

John Steadman's Ratings for 14 Super Bowls

As columnist and sports editor of the *Baltimore News-American,* John Steadman hasn't missed a Super Bowl. The One-to-Four-Star Steadman System is based, he says, on performance on the field, historical importance, and how dull it was. As will be seen, Steadman gave four stars to only two Super Bowls, XIII and XIV. And only one other game, Super Bowl III, with Joe Namath, got as many as three stars. Explains Steadman: "The Jet-Colt game was a bad game, but it was important as a historic happening."

I—*Green Bay 35, Kansas City 10, Jan. 14, 1967, Los Angeles Memorial Coliseum, 61,946. The start of all this super nonsense, and the best pro-football city in America yawned with over 30,000 empty seats. Packer coach Vince Lombardi said he didn't regard the game with as much importance as he placed on his team meeting the Chicago Bears or the Detroit Lions.

II—*Green Bay 33, Oakland 14, Jan. 14, 1968, Miami Orange Bowl, 75,564. Don Chandler kicked four field goals. It was obvious Lombardi's teams had little trouble scoring on the AFL—68 points in two Super Bowls.

III—***New York Jets 16, Baltimore 7, Jan. 12, 1969, Miami Orange Bowl, 75,389. A momentous upset. The fact that Joe Namath didn't accept Lou Michaels' challenge to fight on the Sunday before made it possible for him to predict and produce a shocking result.

IV—*Kansas City 23, Minnesota 7, Jan. 11, 1970, New Orleans Tulane Stadium, 80,562. The only time a president of the United States, Richard Nixon, called a team locker room both before and after the game. He first spoke of his confidence in QB Len Dawson and then congratulated him when it was over.

V—**Baltimore 16, Dallas 13, Jan. 17, 1971, Miami Orange Bowl, 79,204. Fumbles and interceptions made it a comedy of errors, but it held the audience's attention, even if the futility demeaned it as a classic. Jim O'Brien's 32-yard field goal with five seconds left saved all of us from the burden of overtime.

The victory scene for Joe Namath, his dad, and Weeb Ewbank (left).
Barton Silverman

VI—*Dallas 24, Miami 3. Jan. 16, 1972, New Orleans Tulane Stadium, 80,591. Dallas totally dominated. Miami became the only team in Super Bowl history that couldn't score a touchdown.

VII—**Miami 14, Washington 7, Jan. 14, 1973, Los Angeles Memorial Coliseum, 90,182. Garo Yepremian found out he wasn't a passer. The Dolphins accomplished the impossible by becoming the first pro team ever to record a perfect 17-0 season.

VIII—*Miami 24, Minnesota 7, Jan. 13, 1974, Houston Rice Stadium, 71,882. During the week before the game, coach Bud Grant of the Vikings complained about locker-room facilities and even found sparrows in the showers. Larry Csonka powered his way for 145 yards and the noise he created inside the helmets of the Vikings sounded like those same birds singing.

IX—**Pittsburgh 16, Minnesota 6, Jan. 12, 1975, New Orleans Tulane Stadium, 80,997. After 42 years, and all of them losers, owner Art Rooney walked away a champion. The world was smiling with him, and unpretentious Art asked a sportswriter friend, "How's your family?"

X—**Pittsburgh 21, Dallas 17, Jan. 18, 1976, Miami Orange Bowl, 80,187. Terry Bradshaw, knocked unconscious on a blitz, released the ball to Lynn Swann for a 59-yard touchdown on 3rd-and-4 when everyone expected he'd be passing short.

XI—**Oakland 32, Minnesota 14, Jan. 9, 1977, Pasadena Rose Bowl, 103,438. The Raiders ran left behind Gene Upshaw and Art Shell. There was more running room than you'd find on the Santa Ana Freeway.

XII—*Dallas 27, Denver 10, Jan. 15, 1978, New Orleans Superdome, 76,400. Indoors for the first time. The Cowboys forced Craig Morton out of the pocket and invited him to run—which they knew he couldn't do.

XIII—****Pittsburgh 35, Dallas 31, Jan. 21, 1979, Miami Orange Bowl, 78,656. Finally, a game befitting the name Super Bowl. A matchup of the two finest quarterbacks the Super Bowl has seen. Terry Bradshaw and Roger Staubach were in epic form.

XIV—****Pittsburgh 31, Los Angeles 19, Jan. 20, 1980, Pasadena Rose Bowl, 103,985. A Super Bowl so super, it will be the yardstick for measuring those to come.

Mickey Herskowitz's 8 Worst No. 1 Picks in the Pro Football Draft

In addition to writing a sports column for the *Houston Post,* Mickey Herskowitz has co-authored books with Howard Cosell, newsman Dan Rather, and actress Gene Tierney.

1. Jay Berwanger, Chicago Bears—The first No. 1 ever picked, and he refused to report.
2. Joe Heap, New York Giants—Cut in training camp, out of Notre Dame.
3. Bob Fennimore, Chicago Bears
4. Terry Baker, Los Angeles Rams
5. Jack Concannon, Boston Patriots
6. John Matuszak, Houston Oilers
7. Lawrence Elkins, Houston Oilers
8. Jim Plunkett, New England Patriots

Allie Sherman's 10 Left-Handed Quarterbacks

Allie Sherman is the only left-handed quarterback ever to coach a team to three straight championships in the NFL, the New York Giants in 1961, 1962, and 1963. He was a left-handed T-formation quarterback at Brooklyn College, and it was his familiarity with the new-fangled formation, which he learned out of a book, that prompted Greasy Neale to draft him for the Philadelphia Eagles.

The Giants acquired Sherman from the Eagles for the sole purpose of teaching the T formation to their rookie quarterback, Charley Conerly. Currently, Sherman is an executive with Warner Communications, specializing in cable-TV, and he sits on the Board of Directors of the Cosmos of the NASL.

While he admits that left-handed passers look awkward, Sherman says the main reason there are so few in football is "because receivers don't like them. The spin of their ball is different, and it's hard to get used to that spin, unless you play together a lot."

1. Ken Stabler
2. Jim Zorn
3. Frankie Albert
4. Bobby Douglass
5. Jim Del Gaizo
6. Terry Baker
7. David Humm
8. Rick Leach
9. Paul McDonald
10. Allie Sherman

EDITORS' NOTE: The first five are rated for their passing ability. The last five are listed alphabetically. Says Sherman: "Stabler and

12

Zorn are on a par as passers, and they are the best left-handed passers I've seen. Stabler has a great feel and a great release, and his play-calling is excellent. He can throw those 14-yard and 16-yard darts. Zorn is very mobile. He reminds me of a Tarkenton-type quarterback, as well as being an excellent passer. Albert was very clever, a great field general. He didn't throw the ball as well as Stabler and Zorn, but he had an excellent feel for timing, kind of like a left-handed Bobby Layne. I had Douglass in the Senior Bowl. He's a tremendous athlete and has a strong arm, although he was erratic." As for himself, Sherman said: "I don't think I threw enough balls to be rated."

George Halas' 9 Essentials for Winning

George Halas is the only man inducted into the Pro Football Hall of Fame in three categories (player, coach, owner). Not only was he a star on the football field, coach and owner of the Chicago Bears, and a founder of the National Football League, Halas played major league baseball as an outfielder for the New York Yankees. He knows about winning, and losing.

"In searching for players over the past 60 years," Halas says, "I have looked for a fine combination of intelligence and natural ability. But the smartest and most agile player is useless unless he also has what I call the great desire—mental heat, the old zipperoo."

1. Mental aspects of football—"You may have speed, weight, and ability, and all the physical qualifications that are essential to a great athlete. However, men are not machines, and so with the team. There must be some inherent force to drive you forward."
2. Pride and tradition—"It is an advantage to be a member of an organization with great tradition, and it is a responsibility to uphold that tradition."
3. Aggressiveness—"This is the first quality a coach seeks in a man, for without it, he cannot make a contribution to the team. As a candidate for the team it will be to your advantage to show aggressiveness the very moment you step out on the practice field."

Ken Stabler, Oakland's southpaw snake.

Mitchell Reibel

4. Concentration—"It is essential that every candidate know every play precisely, exactly, immediately, and without the slightest doubt as to how it should be executed."
5. Determination—"Some men go through an entire season content to 'fool around,' cut up, wisecrack, and as a result never contribute to the squad. Take a personal pride in having serious determination of purpose to become the very best football player possible."
6. Leadership—"Every organization must have leadership. In football, that leadership is in the captain, the players, and the coaches. Many players resent criticism from the coaches and captain merely because they fail to understand the real reason for such criticism. We are all working for the common end—a championship football team."
7. Reliability—"Reliability is one of your greatest single assets. It is the quality that every employer seeks. It is the quality that all men should cultivate."
8. Confidence—"Confidence is belief in yourself and your team that you can achieve victory by hard, intelligent fighting."
9. Cooperation—"Any man going out for football must bury his selfish interest. A team is not the product of one player, one man, one group. It is your duty to yourself, to your friends, and to your team to keep this foremost in mind at all times."

SOURCE: *Halas by Halas,* by George Halas, with Gwen Morgan and Arthur Veysey (McGraw-Hill).

Bum Phillips' 7 Rules for Coaching 45 Large Men

O. A. "Bum" Phillips is the tobacco-chewing, cowboy-boots-wearing coach of the Houston Oilers, whose success in the NFL belies his reputation as a wit. Noted for his down-home humor, Phillips came from the small town of Orange, Tex., and rose from high school coach to top man of the Oilers in 1974.

1. "I never scrimmage Oilers against Oilers. . . . What for? Houston isn't on our schedule."
2. "I seldom drill players more than 65 or 75 minutes. . . . If I want more conditioning, I wait 'til practice is over and then I run 'em."

Bum Phillips is home on the range.

George Gojkovich

3. "I demand effort and extra effort. . . . If you don't like my attitude, see your friendly player rep."
4. "I expect daily improvement from my players. . . . A football season is like a football game, you try to be better in the fourth quarter."
5. "I invite families to our Saturday practice sessions. . . . everybody, wives, kids, dogs."
6. "I expect players to be self-motivated, not driven. . . . You can't win today by embarrassing players. If I played for a guy who shouted at me, I'd sock him."
7. "I never solicit advice from my wife, Helen. . . . I don't help her cook and she don't help me coach."

SOURCE: *He Ain't No Bum*, by O. A. "Bum" Phillips and Ray Buck (Jordan & Co.).

Herman L. Masin's 13 Most Meaningful Innovations in Football History

Herman L. Masin is editor of *Scholastic Coach* magazine.

1. Pop Warner—Single and double wings
2. Knute Rockne—Notre Dame box
3. Ox DaGrosa—5-3 defense
4. Shaugnessy/Jones/Halas—The modern T
5. Steve Owen—Umbrella defense
6. Don Faurot—Split T
7. Greasy Neale—Eagle defense (4-3)
8. Bud Wilkinson—Oklahoma defense (3-4)
9. Paul Brown—Total organization
10. Sid Gillman—Film breakdowns
11. Tom Nugent—I formation
12. Frank Broyles—Belly play
13. Darrell Royal—Wishbone T

Ted Emery's All-Time Gator Bowl Team

Ted Emery, formerly Sports Information Director at Dartmouth, and Public Relations Director of the New York Titans (later the Jets), is currently Public Relations Director for the Jacksonville-based Gator Bowl.

OFFENSE

E—Fred Biletnikoff, Florida State, 1965
E—Ron Sellers, Florida State, 1967

Knute Rockne is a Notre Dame legend. *UPI*

T—Jack Bush, Georgia, 1948
T—Jim Stuckey, Clemson, 1978
G—Gary Bugenhagen, Syracuse, 1966
G—Bob Ward, Maryland, 1950
C—Maxie Baughan, Georgia Tech, 1960
QB—Archie Manning, Mississippi, 1970; Matt Cavanaugh, Pittsburgh, 1977
HB—Floyd Little, Syracuse, 1966
HB—Lu Gambino, Maryland, 1948
FB—Larry Csonka, Syracuse, 1966
Punter—Nick Vidnovic, North Carolina, 1971
Place kicker—Obed Ariri, Clemson, 1977

DEFENSE

E—Dave Robinson, Penn State, 1962
E—Ross Browner, Notre Dame, 1976
T—Mark Cooney, Colorado, 1972
T—Randy Holloway, Pittsburgh, 1977
LB—Dave Sicks, Air Force, 1963
LB—Tom Cousineau, Ohio State, 1978
LB—Sammy Green, Florida, 1975
CB—Larry Willingham, Auburn, 1970
CB—Jim Brechbiel, Maryland, 1975
Safety—Roger Wehrli, Missouri, 1968
Safety—Joe Restic, Notre Dame, 1976

Adds Emery: "Although I have seen most of these players in action in person, others have been seen only in the re-run of past Football Classics highlight films. This is, however, a good representative list of the players who have performed in games here since 1946."

V

Say It Ain't So

Jerry Coleman's 14 Best (But Not Only) Malaprops

For seven years, Jerry Coleman, former New York Yankee star second baseman and war hero, broadcast the games of the San Diego Padres. Before that, he broadcast the games of the Yankees and California Angels. In a shocking move, the Padres named Coleman their manager for the 1980 season, denying, however, that they did so to avoid further pollution of the air waves in southern California. Coleman will be missed for his on-air comments, such as the following:

1. "We're all sad to see Glenn Beckert leave. Before he goes, though, I hope he stops by so we can kiss him good-bye. He's that kind of guy."
2. "On the mound is Randy Jones, the left-hander with the Karl Marx hairdo."
3. "There's a fly ball deep to center field. Winfield is going back, back . . . he hits his head against the wall. It's rolling toward second base."
4. "He slides into second with a standup double."
5. "Rich Folkers is throwing up in the bullpen."
6. "Grubb goes back, back . . . he's under the warning track, and he makes the play."
7. "The big ballpark can do it all."
8. "Young Frank Pastore may have just pitched the biggest victory of 1979, maybe the biggest victory of the year."

9. "If Rose's streak was still intact, with that single to left, the fans would be throwing babies out of the upper deck."
10. "Hrabosky looks fierce in that Fu Manchu haircut."
11. "Bob Davis is wearing his hair differently this year, short and with curls, like Randy Jones wears. I think you call it a Frisbee."
12. "Next up for the Cardinals is Barry, Carry, Garry Templeton."
13. "Hendrick simply lost that sun-blown pop-up."
14. "Those amateur umpires are certainly flexing their fangs tonight."

Ted Patterson's 8 Famous and Not So Famous Sportscasting Bloopers

Baltimore sports announcer, historian of sports broadcasting, and collector of memorabilia Ted Patterson has written extensively about radio and TV sports. He is author of *Orioles Silver Anniversary Trivia Book.*

1. In a class by itself as the biggest boo-boo was Clem McCarthy's call in the 1947 Preakness. McCarthy, broadcasting in his typical, pebbly, staccato fashion, lost the horses in the stretch. From his poor vantage point at ground level, he announced Jet Pilot the winner when it was Faultless. Realizing his mistake, Clem artfully corrected himself by saying: "I made a mistake, somehow mixing my horses. Well, Babe Ruth struck out. I'm in distinguished company."
2. Just about any game that Bill Stern ever broadcast. An admitted showman with little regard for accuracy, Stern once arrived late for a Cotton Bowl broadcast and had the players and teams reversed for half of the first quarter. If a game was one-sided, he didn't give the score. Once, while broadcasting an Old Oaken Bucket game between Purdue and Indiana, he said late in the game: "The score is Indiana 34, Purdue 11. If Indiana can hold this lead for the next 48 seconds, they'll win the game." If he had the wrong man running for a touchdown, Bill would simply have the ball lateralled to the right man.
3. Just about any game that Harry Wismer ever broadcast. His broadcasts of long touchdown runs were the lengthiest on record. By the time the runner meandered his way from one

Clem McCarthy broadcast the Kentucky Derby for more than two decades.
NBC-Ted Patterson Collection

end of the field to the other, Harry had the carrier running past some of the biggest names in politics and show business, all friends of his. In one of his many "Game of the Century" broadcasts in the 1940s, Harry screamed, "He's at the 40, the 45, the 50, the 55, the 65 . . ."

Bill Stern made a career of passing fiction for fact.
NBC-Bill Stern Collection

4. One candid adjective got CBS's immortal Ted Husing into trouble at Harvard. In the 1931 Yale-Harvard football game, he referred to Barry Wood's play as "putrid." The Harvard administration banned him from future broadcasts of their games. The ban was eventually lifted.
5. Graham McNamee of early NBC fame was noted for his descriptions of everything but the game he was broadcasting.

Veteran baseball scribe Fred Lieb remembers the 1926 World Series in which McNamee requested an interview with National League President John Heydler. McNamee gave a flowery introduction, saying his guest had made his mark in politics as governor of Pennsylvania. Unfortunately, McNamee was confusing Heydler with John K. Tener, who had served as league president eight years earlier. Making a swift recovery, McNamee announced, "My slip. It's not John K. Tener, but John A. Heydler, who also has a great background."

6. Fred Hoey, who broadcast Red Sox and Boston Braves baseball in the 1930s, often got tongue-tied, which resulted in such utterances as "Hello, Fred Hoey, everybody speaking." Once, after a Jimmy Foxx homer, he shouted, "Homer hit a Foxx." One of Hoey's favorites was, "They're off and rocking at Runningham."
7. Howard Cosell, who needs no introduction, says in 50 words what could be said in 10. He hit a superfluous peak during a game in which he said, "Let us reflect back nostalgically on the past."
8. Curt Gowdy, in referring to a player's home state, said, "He was born originally in . . ."

17 One-to-Five Liners That Are Hanging Around Out There Waiting to Be Said

1. Ilie Nastase, after changing his shorts *al fresco* at the 1979 National Open: "I just felt like dropping a little behind in the match."
2. Bob Lemon, upon being demoted to an administrative job by the Yankees: "They gave me an office I couldn't refuse."
3. Woody Hayes, upon accepting the Alumni Association Award for Building Character: "This is a great moment in the history of mankind, and I accept it humbly in the name of my three guiding angels—General Patton, Strangler Lewis, and Attila the Hun."
4. Kevin Loughery, on the NBA rule restricting coaches to a limited area on the sidelines: "It may throw us off course, but never off curse."
5. Joe Torre, on how he feels about having a woman owner who's always running out on the field to shake his hand: "I'll begin worrying when she starts taking showers with the guys."

6. Arnold Palmer: "Even after my wife adjusted my grip, it took me three tries to put a spoon in my coffee cup."
7. George Steinbrenner, after the assassination of Abraham Lincoln: "I've hired a special stage coach to take the team to the funeral and get them back to New York in time for a twi-night doubleheader, because Abe's wife told me he would have wanted it that way."
8. Leon Spinks: "Can anyone tell me where I can get some dental floss that's six inches wide?"
9. Steve Ross, owner of the Cosmos: "We've just signed Doc Halliday, and we'll never lose a shoot-out again."
10. Jayne Kennedy, on the secret of her success with the football scoreboard: "Tight blouses and big cue cards."
11. Howard Cosell, at any funeral: "When the Big Coach in the Sky (No. 1 in your program) looks down upon our departed brother, he will say it like it is, and as I told you at the top of the show, 'Dandy Don Twin D. Schwartz, No. 74 of hallowed memory, you were some kind of ballplayer.' "
12. Bobby Knight, brusquely rejecting a covey of female sportswriters: "Me Tarzan, you Janes."
13. Billy Martin, on his relationship with Reggie Jackson: "It has gone from bitter to wurst."
14. Red Auerbach, after the courts soaked the Lakers $3.3 million for Kermit Washington's "act of self-defense" on Rudy Tomjanovich's face: "In August, the offense is always ahead of the defense."
15. Roone Arledge; "NBC may have beaten us to the Olympics, but we beat 'em to the Demolition Camel Derby in Erg Chech."
16. Lee Marvin: "When the One Great Scorer comes to write against your name, it won't matter whether you won or lost but how you paid the dame."
17. Joe Garagiola: "Does Charlie Finley have any redeeming social values?"

SOURCE: Herman L. Masin, editor, *Scholastic Coach* magazine.

Washington was never the same after Casey Stengel—flanked by Mickey Mantle and Ted Williams—testified before the Senate Anti-Trust and Monopoly Subcommittee.

UPI

Harold Rosenthal's 10 Most Memorable Baseball Quotes

As a baseball writer for the defunct *New York Herald-Tribune,* Harold Rosenthal always had an ear for a good quote.

1. "He's dead at the present time."—Casey Stengel, referring to a departed comrade-in-arms.
2. "The road will make a bum of the best of them."—Anonymous. First believed to have been used by Hannibal on his elephant-crossing of the Alps, in his futile attack on Rome.
3. "Don't give him nuthin' good to hit, but don't walk him."—Curious advice given by a harassed manager to a harassed pitcher in a tough situation. First recorded mention came from Harry Wright, manager of Providence the year Old Hoss Radbourn won 60 games.
4. "No one should be able to steal second base on a left-handed pitcher."—This quote is attributed to Branch Rickey, one of

the true geniuses produced by the game. He was talking about the advantages of a left-hander, who always has the runner in view. Rickey said nothing about stealing on right-handed catchers, of which he was one. Catching for the new York Yankees, he gave up what is still a record of 14 stolen bases in one game. He claimed he had a sore arm that day.

5. "No one was ever paid more than he was worth."—This is a comparatively recent addition, coming after the owners, in their rush to give the store away, started handing out $300,000 salaries to 12-game winners when they became available as free agents. The quote is attributed to pitcher Wayne Garland, who went from the Orioles to the Indians. When he failed to produce, he said: "I didn't ask for the money, they offered it to me. No one was ever paid more than he was worth." The kid's right.
6. "Always take two."—James Parnell Dawson, the late *New York Times* baseball writer, advising a young writer on how to act when the post-dinner cigars are handed out.
7. "All the Reds have to do is win one more game each week to be right in there for the pennant race."—Gabe Paul when he was boss of the Cincinnati Reds and they were a chronic second-division club. This is in the same category as "If my grandmother had a beard and wore Confederate gray, she'd have been General Beauregard."
8. "Only half the lies they tell about the Irish are true."—The late Walter O'Malley, who built an empire that produced the first three-million attendance ball club, got tired of people telling him how he had stolen half of Los Angeles when he moved the Dodgers westward, and used to fall back upon this County Donegal line to end the discussion. If it hadn't been O'Malley building a ballpark within howitzer range of downtown City Hall, it probably would have been some chemical company with a plant capable of poisoning the surrounding 350,000 square miles. Instead, the customers got Sandy Koufax, Don Drysdale, and Maury Wills.
9. "Tip half dollars."—Joe DiMaggio in the days when a quarter was a substantial gratuity and ball players were leaving 15-cent tips at dinner.
10. "Never underestimate the stupidity of the American public." —Edward T. Murphy, a pre-World War II baseball writer in New York, who was upset by the public's acceptance of the shenanigans and all-around perfidy of the baseball owners.

Murphy quit what used to be regarded as a highly attractive job as a traveling writer and went inside to work on the desk with the advent of night baseball, saying, "I don't want to sit around like a burglar all day, waiting for it to get dark so I can go to work."

Red Holzman's 6 Basic Rules on Life

Basketball coach, cigar-smoker, connoisseur of fine wine, and philosopher, William "Red" Holzman of the New York Knicks is the second winningest coach in NBA history. He brought the Knicks their only two league titles. He lives by an old family philosophy, handed down from his father. "My father used to say, 'If I live, I'll do it tomorrow, if not, I'll do it the next day.' "

1. A broad-beamed bus driver is a good bus driver.
2. Never get your hair cut by a bald-headed barber. He has no respect for your hair.
3. Never take medical advice from a waiter.
4. Never talk about money with your wife at night when you're going to bed.
5. Never accidentally raise your hand or point your finger to make a point when the check is coming.
6. It's not hard to get up early in the morning if you have no place to go.

John Halligan's 5 Favorite Hockey Quotes

John Halligan is director of public relations for the New York Rangers and, as such, is always on the lookout for things said about his sport. If it's said about hockey, Halligan will hear about it.

1. "You hockey puck!"—Don Rickles
2. "If hockey fights were fixed, I'd be in more of them."—Rod Gilbert
3. "Gentlemen, I have nothing to say. Any questions?"—Phil Watson (to reporters during the customary post-game interview)
4. "I went to the fights the other night and a hockey game broke out."—Rodney Dangerfield
5. "If you can't beat 'em in the alley, you can't beat 'em on the ice."—Connie Smythe

A New Yorker who starred as a player at CCNY and later with Rochester in the NBL and NBA, Red Holzman made his greatest impact as coach of the New York Knicks.

UPI

Graig Nettles' 7 Best One-Liners

The Yankees' Gold Glove third baseman is not only quick with his mitt, he's also quick with his wit. He takes pride in coming up with the subtle one-liner that best fits the occasion. His humor is sharp and sarcastic, and sometimes at his own expense. For example, he has written on the back of his glove, "E-5," the baseball scorer's shorthand for "Error—third base."

1. On what it's like to play for the Yankees: "Most kids, when they're growing up, want to play in the major leagues or be in the circus. I'm lucky, I got to do both."
2. On the advantages of playing in New York: "You get to see Reggie Jackson play every day." On the disadvantages of playing in New York: "You get to see Reggie Jackson play every day."
3. When former teammate Sparky Lyle was traded the year after he won the American League Cy Young Award: "Sparky went from Cy Young to Sayonara."
4. Frustrated because he was often placed sixth or seventh in the Yankee batting order: "I don't strike out often enough to bat fourth."
5. Still frustrated at batting sixth or seventh in the Yankee batting order: "It's a good thing Babe Ruth still isn't here. If he was, George [Steinbrenner] would have him bat seventh and say he's overweight."
6. After being fined for missing a "Welcome Home" luncheon: "If the Yankees want somebody to play third base, they've got me. If they want someone to attend banquets, they can get Georgie Jessel."
7. On an airplane trip: "We've got a problem. Luis Tiant wants to use the bathroom and it says no foreign objects in the toilet."

10 Quotations from Chairman Fred Shero

By nature, Fred Shero, general manager-coach of the New York Rangers, is a man of few words. Many of his words, in fact, come in the form of sayings scrawled on dressing-room blackboards and are designed to motivate his team. As the man with the second-best coaching percentage in the history of the National Hockey League and one of the most highly acclaimed hockey authorities in the world, Shero is clearly a man with something to say. Herewith, 10 Fred Sheroisms, culled from various sources.

1. "Always behave like a duck—calm and unruffled on the surface—paddle like hell underneath."
2. "There are things I do for my players that I wouldn't do for my sons."
3. "Take the shortest route to the puck carrier—and arrive in ill humor."
4. "Experience is the name we give our mistakes."
5. "To avoid criticism: say nothing, do nothing, be nothing."
6. "The only people not under stress are dead."
7. "Temptation rarely comes in working hours. It's in their leisure time that men are made or marred."
8. "I do not believe you can perform today's business with yesterday's methods and expect to be in business tomorrow."
9. "Earn the respect of your players, don't demand it."
10. "It's what you learn after you know it all that counts."

5 Comments by Sports Figures, Having to Do with the Meaning of Life

1. "A tie is like kissing your sister."—Bear Bryant.
2. "Football is not a contact sport, it's a collision sport. Dancing is a contact sport."—Duffy Daugherty.
3. "Some people who don't say ain't, ain't eating."—Dizzy Dean.
4. "First the legs go, then the reflexes go, then your friends go." —Willie Pep, former featherweight champion of the world.
5. "Happiness is a first-class pad, good wheels, an understanding manager, and a little action."—Bo Belinsky, former major league pitcher and playboy.

SOURCE: Mickey Herskowitz, *Houston Post.*

VI

Fore!

Arnold Palmer's Best 18 Golf Holes

1. The Country Club (Composite Course), Brookline, Mass., par 4, 11th hole.
2. Southern Hills CC, Tulsa, Okla., par 4, 12th hole.
3. Laurel Valley GC, Ligonier, Pa., par 4, 18th hole.
4. Oakmont CC, Oakmont, Pa., par 4, 15th hole.
5. Cypress Point Club, Pebble Beach, Calif., par 4, 17th hole.
6. Oakland Hills CC, Birmingham, Mich., par 4, 16th hole.
7. Pebble Beach Golf Links, Pebble Beach, Calif., par 4, 8th hole.
8. The Champions GC, Houston, Tex., par 4, 14th hole.
9. Merion GC (East Course), Ardmore, Pa., par 3, 13th hole.
10. Bay Hill Club, Orlando, Fla., par 3, 17th hole.
11. Augusta National GC, Augusta, Ga., par 3, 12th hole.
12. Medinah CC (No. 3 Course), Medinah, Ill., par 3, 2nd hole.
13. Baltusrol GC (Lower Course), Springfield, N.J., par 3, 4th hole.
14. Firestone CC (South Course), Akron, Ohio, par 5, 16th hole.
15. Augusta National GC, Augusta, Ga., par 5, 13th hole.
16. Seminole GC, Palm Beach, Fla., par 5, 15th hole.
17. Cherry Hills CC, Denver, Colo., par 5, 17th hole.
18. Olympic Club (Lake Course), San Francisco, Calif., par 5, 16th hole.

SOURCE: *Arnold Palmer's Best 54 Golf Holes,* by Arnold Palmer with Bob Drum (Doubleday).

Joe Schwendeman's 10 Most and Memorable Holes-in-One

Currently director of communications for the USGA, Joe Schwendeman covered golf for the *Philadelphia Bulletin* and *Philadelphia Inquirer* for 20 years. He says, "All golfers should tip their caps to *Golf Digest* magazine, which, in recent years, has become the clearing-house for holes-in-one. The editors have noted the proliferation of aces. In 1979, the total topped 29,000 made in the United States alone. Recently, the magazine figured the odds against an average golfer making an ace are 10,738 to one. On the PGA tour, where the best players in the world compete, the odds are 3,708 to one. On the Ladies PGA circuit, those figures are 4,648 to one."

1. Amateur Norman Manley, of Long Beach, Calif., has recorded 44 holes-in-one, and he's still going strong. This is believed to be the most aces scored by any golfer.
2. Professional Art Wall, a Masters champion, has scored 42. No other professional has knocked in as many. Sam Snead, for example, has 24; Jack Nicklaus, 10; and Arnold Palmer, 9.
3. Most memorable: Mary Kent scored an ace in 1978, hitting a five-iron shot into the hole on a 170-yarder at West Palm Beach. This was extremely noteworthy because Mary weighed only 97 pounds and was 90 years old. "That happens when you love golf and say your prayers every night," she explained.
4. Third-grade pupil Rebecca Ann Chase, the eight-year-old daughter of a Dallas high school golf coach, received some instructions in the game, and when it came time for her to go out and play, she aced the very first hole. It was 100 yards long and she used a cut-down three wood.
5. Dick McCelland used all the angles in scoring an ace in 1978 in Fairfax, Calif. His errant shot struck a golf cart parked to the left of the green, then bounced off the shoulder of a waiting player, fell to the green, and rolled into the cup. He marked a "1" on his scorecard while everyone else fell over laughing.
6. Bob Hope's third hole-in-one (he had scored four through 1979) was made with a seven iron on the 150-yard eighth hole

Bob Hope plays the eternal comic in a charity match in London in 1953, but as a serious golfer he has scored four holes-in-one.

UPI

at Bob O'Link Golf Club in Highland Park, Ill. His group that day included Joe Louis and Fred Astaire. The ball went into the cup on the fly, and, for once, Hope didn't have a wisecrack. He said, "It's a wonder it didn't bounce out."

7. Bill Voigt, of South St. Paul, Minn., made a hole-in-one in 1969 on the Phelan Park course, but it didn't count. The green is on a high plateau, and what Voigt did not know when he hit the ball was that workmen were installing a watering line on the green and that a temporary green had been placed next to the original. Voigt's shot, however, went into the hole that remained on the original.
8. Arnold Palmer has nine aces to his credit, but he also scored one that did not go on his scorecard as a "1." One day a few years ago, while playing the 17th hole of his Bay Hill course, Arnie missed the green with his two iron, and the ball splashed short, into the pond. That's a stroke-and-distance penalty, two strokes. Then he holed out his next shot for a "3."
9. Robert Mutera is generally credited with scoring the longest hole-in-one, a prodigious 447 yards. It was made in 1965 on a course in Omaha that has an appropriate name for the feat: Miracle Hills Golf Club.
10. Gene Sarazen made a hole-in-one that warmed the hearts of all nostalgia buffs in the game. Playing in the 1973 British Open—on the 50th anniversary of his playing that tournament—Gene aced the famous "postage stamp hole," so named because the green on the Troon course in Scotland is so small. The ace was recorded on BBC television and was also made in the presence of two other former British Open titlists, Fred Daly and Max Faulkner. It also was Gene's last British Open.

The 10 Greatest Golf Courses in the United States

(Listed Alphabetically)

1. Augusta National GC, Augusta, Ga., 6,980 yards, par 72, home of the Masters Tournament.
2. Cypress Point Club, Pebble Beach, Calif., 6,464 yards, par 72.

Arnold Palmer plays out of a trap on San Francisco's Olympic Club course in the 1966 U.S. Open.

UPI

3. Merion GC (East Course), Ardmore, Pa., 6,498 yards, par 70, site of the 1981 U.S. Open.
4. Oakmont CC, Oakmont, Pa., 6,938 yards, par 72.
5. Olympic Club (Lake Course), San Francisco, Calif., 6,669 yards, par 71.
6. Pebble Beach Golf Links, Pebble Beach, Calif., 6,815 yards, par 72.
7. Pine Valley GC, Clementon, N.J., 6,765 yards, par 70.
8. Seminole GC, North Palm Beach, Fla., 6,898 yards, par 72.
9. Southern Hills CC, Tulsa, Okla., 7,037 yards, par 71.
10. Winged Foot GC (West Course), Mamaroneck, N.Y., 6,956 yards, par 72.

SOURCE: *Golf Digest.*

6 Tips from the Pros on How to Speed Up Golf Play

1. Tom Watson: "I didn't become a leading money-winner by playing slowly. Be ready to hit when it's your turn."
2. Ben Crenshaw: "Don't take Mulligans. Do your practicing before the round."
3. Lee Trevino: "Don't stand on the green after holing out. Mark your score on the next tee."
4. Lee Elder: "If you play out of a golf car, take two or three clubs with you so you'll be ready when it's your turn."
5. Deane Beman: "If the following foursome is pressing you, wave them through and then speed up."
6. Fuzzy Zoeller: "Line up your putt while someone else is putting."

SOURCE: *Golf Digest*

Danny Lawler's Top 10 and Second 12 Golf-Playing Baseball Players

Called "the golf pro of the major leaguers," Danny Lawler does public relations work for Izod sportswear (the alligator company). For years, he was golf pro at Rock Ridge Country Club, in Newtown, Conn. He has taught a wide assortment of celebrities, from baseball players to astronauts. Among his pupils are Don Rickles, Joe Garagiola, Vince Scully, and Bob Newhart. Lawler is credited with introducing the golf glove to baseball, and he says the first to use gloves when hitting, now used by almost every batter, were Birdie Tebbetts and Bobby Thompson. According to Lawler, "pitchers make the best golfers because they have a better feel in their fingers."

THE TOP 10

1. Peanuts Lowery—Best pressure-playing golfer of all.
2. Ken Harrelson—Strong hands and accurate.
3. Jim Rice—Shoots in the middle 70s. Strong off tees and on long iron shots.
4. Jim Hearn—Long off tees; great short game.
5. Ralph Terry—Very accurate with middle irons and approach shots.
6. Jack Russell—Good all-around game.
7. Tommy John—Best temperament of all. Shoots in the mid-70s.
8. Alvin Dark—Baseball players' golf tourney champion several times. Good around greens. Always fought a duck hook.
9. Al Lopez—Uncanny with the putter.
10. Jack Sanford—Very long off tees and on middle irons.

THE SECOND 12

1. Phil Rizzuto—Great agility, consistent, all-around, but needs better putting technique.
2. Don Zimmer—Hits missile shots.
3. Mel Ott—A master with the Texas wedge (a little run-up shot).
4. Joe DiMaggio—If he practiced, he could have been a pro. Has the best grip, including the pros, I've ever seen.
5. Birdie Tebbetts—A fine golfer who could beat you psychologically.
6. Don Drysdale—Very good with his long game.
7. Ed Lopat—Steady Eddie, and that's how he played.
8. Bob Kennedy—One of the best thinking players.
9. Mickey Mantle—Could hit 300 to 350 off the tee, a 3-handicap golfer.
10. Sammy Byrd—The first baseball player to become a pro. Exceptionally good all-around.
11. Whitey Ford—Great feel in the hands. He could come up with a payoff shot any time, the way he did in the pinch in baseball.

12. Yogi Berra—Plays in the low 80s. Hits his shots right-handed until he gets to the wedge and putter, and these he makes left-handed.

Hubert Mizell's 5 Worst Failures for a Golfer

Hubert Mizell, who is guilty of all five failures on the golf course, is also guilty of writing an informative and entertaining sports column for the *St. Petersburg* (Fla.) *Times.*

1. Lack of concentration
2. Lack of tempo
3. Lifting the head
4. Too quick on the backswing
5. Bad grip

Yogi Berra was a left-handed hitter in baseball, but drives right in golf.
American Airlines

VII

The City Game

Nancy Lieberman's 10 Greatest Professional Basketball Players (Men) of All Time

Nancy Lieberman was the youngest member of the United States' 1976 Olympic women's basketball squad. She led Old Dominion University to the 1979 women's national championship and was expected to lead the U.S. Olympic entry in Moscow. Her list includes only players she has seen play.

1. Jerry West—A great shooter and clutch performer. If you needed the basket, here was the man to do it.
2. Oscar Robertson—A fantastic floor leader and all-around player. He rarely made a mistake.
3. Wilt Chamberlain—The most dominant offensive player of his time. Strength, size, and ability.
4. Elgin Baylor—He could do things with the ball that nobody else could: moves, hang time, shooting, rebounding.
5. John Havlicek—Great all-around player, with or without the ball. Could complement any teammate on the court. Great ball sense; unselfish. A quiet player who kills you.
6. Walt Frazier—Fantastic ability to force opponents to turn the ball over. Great defensive player, as well as offensive. Could run any basketball team because of his leadership on the court.

The Los Angeles Lakers' Jerry West led the NBA in broken noses, among other things.

Darryl Norenberg

7. Paul Westphal—Can do anything he wants to with the ball. Uncanny ability to get shots off on the drive or outside. Great passer.
8. Bill Russell—Most dominant player of all time. Could singlehandedly change the opposition's offense from coming near the goal. Extraordinary shot blocker. Great desire and heart.
9. Dave DeBusschere—This man had the desire that few have had. His rebounding and defensive ability were, without question, fabulous. But the things he did during the course of the game that never showed up in the statistics made him the great player he was.
10. Julius Erving—The most exciting player of all time. What Baylor couldn't do, Julius invented. Great all-around ability. Can fly through the air with moves never before seen. Great rebounder and scorer.

The 2 Most Smashing Backboard Shootouts

1. Boston, November 5, 1946—Chuck Connors, who would later star in *The Rifleman* and other TV and screen productions, played briefly as a first baseman for the Brooklyn Dodgers (1949) and the Chicago Cubs (1951), but he made his mark in basketball as a member of the Boston Celtics when they played the Chicago Stags at the Boston Arena. The Celtics were in the newly formed Basketball Association of America (forerunner of the NBA).

   "The game would have been at the Boston Garden," recalled Connors, "but there was a rodeo at the garden, so we were booked at the Arena. We were taking our warm-up shots before the game, and I threw one up—maybe I was 30 feet out—and the next thing I knew the glass backboard was shattered. I didn't think I threw it that hard."

   The game was delayed half an hour while someone borrowed the basket and backboard from the Garden, and the Stags beat the Celtics, 57-55. The 6-7 Connors couldn't recall whether he made any better shots that night, and his coach, Honey Russell, said "They should give Chuck a bill for the broken backboard."
2. Kansas City, November 13, 1979—Darryl Dawkins of the Philadelphia 76ers soared high for one of his patented dunk

Julius Erving's acrobatics are matched only in the circus.

Rich Pilling

NEW

shots against the Kansas City Kings, and slammed the ball through the basket with such force that he shattered the glass backboard. For good measure, the 6–11, 258-pound center bent the support pole. Kansas City lost the backboard, but won the game, 110–103, and John Begzos, the Kings' general manager, vowed he'd send the bill to the 76ers.

Dr. James Naismith invented the game.

Basketball Hall of Fame

25 Memorable Dates in the History of Basketball

1. December, 1891—James Naismith, an instructor at the School for Christian Workers (now Springfield College), in Springfield, Mass., invents the game of basketball.
2. January 15, 1892—First printed basketball rules appear in the *Triangle,* a paper at the School for Christian Workers.
3. March 11, 1892—First publicly played game of basketball is held between students and teachers at the School for Christian Workers. The students won, 5-1.
4. 1893—Smith College becomes the first women's school to play basketball.
5. January 16, 1896—The University of Chicago and the University of Iowa meet in Iowa City to play the first college game with five players on a side. Chicago won, 15-12.
6. 1898—First professional league is formed and called the National Basketball League.
7. December 29, 1934—First college doubleheader played at Madison Square Garden, in New York City. NYU defeated Notre Dame, 25-18, and Westminster beat St. John's, 37-33.
8. August, 1936—Basketball played for the first time as an Olympic sport.
9. 1937—Center jump after each score is eliminated.
10. March 28, 1939—The University of Oregon defeats Ohio State, 46-33, to win the first NCAA basketball championship.
11. February 28, 1940—First televised basketball game, featuring a doubleheader from Madison Square Garden, Pitt vs. Fordham and NYU vs. Georgetown.
12. June 6, 1946—Basketball Association of America is founded.
13. November 1, 1946—Basketball Association of America begins play as the New York Knickerbockers defeat the Toronto Huskies, 68-66, in Toronto.
14. August, 1949—The Basketball Association of America and National Basketball League merge to become the National Basketball Association.
15. 1950—Charles Cooper of Duquesne University is the first black drafted into the National Basketball Association.
16. March 2, 1951—First NBA All-Star Game is played in Boston. East beats West, 111-94.
17. October 30, 1954—The 24-second clock is used for the first time in an NBA game. Rochester defeats Boston, 98-95, in Rochester.

18. March 2, 1962—Wilt Chamberlain scores 100 points against the New York Knicks, at Hershey, Pa., to lead the Philadelphia Warriors to a 169-147 victory.
19. 1963—Walter Kennedy succeeds Maurice Podoloff as commissioner of the National Basketball Association, becoming the second person to hold the position.
20. February 17, 1968—Basketball Hall of Fame opens in Springfield, Mass.
21. 1967—American Basketball Association begins its first season, with George Mikan serving as commissioner.
22. May 5, 1969—The Boston Celtics win their 11th NBA championship in 13 years, climaxing the end of the Bill Russell Era.
23. January 19, 1974—Notre Dame breaks UCLA's 88-game winning streak at Notre Dame, 71-70.
24. August, 1974—Moses Malone signs with the Utah Stars of the American Basketball Association to become the first professional player in modern times to go directly from high school to the pro ranks.
25. June 1, 1975—Larry O'Brien succeeds Walter Kennedy as commissioner of the National Basketball Association.

SOURCE: Jerry Healy, Promotion Director, the Basketball Hall of Fame.

3 Living Members of the Basketball Hall of Fame Who Are Older Than the Sport Itself

Dr. James Naismith first put up his peach basket in December, 1891. Three men named to the Basketball Hall of Fame in Springfield, Mass., were born before that time.

1. Max Friedman—Captain and coach of the Cleveland Rosenblums, born in New York City, July 12, 1889.
2. Maurice Podoloff—First president of both the ABA and NBA, born August 18, 1890.
3. Elmer H. Ripley—A member of the Original Celtics and coach at Columbia, Yale, Notre Dame, Georgetown, and Army, born July 21, 1891.

The Only 6 Players to Make the All-American High School Basketball Team 3 Times

1. Jerry Lucas (Middletown, Ohio), 1956, 1957, 1958
2. Lew Alcindor (Power Memorial, New York, N.Y.), 1963, 1964, 1965
3. Eugene Banks (West Philadelphia, Pa.), 1975, 1976, 1977
4. Albert King (Fort Hamilton, Brooklyn, N.Y.), 1975, 1976, 1977
5. Wayne McKoy (Long Island Lutheran, Brookfield, N.Y.), 1975, 1976, 1977
6. Earl Jones (Mt. Hope, W. Va., and Springarn, Washington, D.C.), 1978, 1979, 1980

SOURCE: Bruce Weber, *Scholastic Coach* magazine.

Mel Greenberg's 15 Major Developments, 12 Greatest Players, and 14 Greatest Coaches in Women's Basketball Over the Past Decade

Mel Greenberg, of the *Philadelphia Inquirer,* is an expert and historian on women's basketball. He says: "Women's basketball's greatest growth has been in the last decade. In that time, it has gained national acceptance to the point no one says former UCLA All-America Ann Meyers can't play basketball, she just cannot play the NBA brand.

"Listing the greatest developments, players, and coaches for the last 10 years is actually to list them for all time—apologies to Babe Didrikson. The sport's growth has been so dramatic, however, that 1970–75 compares to 1976–79, the way Babe Ruth compares to Hank Aaron. Many of today's players would fare well in one-on-one competition against the early players. Still, those contestants must be given credit as great players of their time.

"For example: Immaculata's Theresa Grentz would have trouble handling Old Dominion's Inge Nissen at center today. In 1972–74, Grentz was the dominant player, listed in national magazines as 'the female Bill Walton.' Basketball's 'Big Woman' was 5-11. Nissen, 6-5, and one of the best centers around, was overshadowed on her own team by 6–8 freshman Anne Donovan."

Delta State's Lusia Harris played a major role in the women's hoop movement.

Richard Lee

DEVELOPMENTS

1. West Chester State Hosts the First National Invitational College Tournament, 1969—It was the first time college women squads competed in a national tournament without AAU teams. Out of the early success came the impetus to form the Association for Intercollegiate Athletics for Women (AIAW), today's governing body for women just like the NCAA, which regulates the men.
2. Five-Player Rules Voted to Become Official, February, 1971—The change from the old six-on-six play made the sport exciting to watch. If it weren't for this development, the majority of today's games would still be played at 4 P.M. before empty stands in the girl's gym.
3. The AIAW National Tournament Is Held at Queens College, N.Y., March, 1973—The event came to the big city for the first time, and the move paid off in instant dividends. The competition received national media attention, including a centerfold pictorial display in the *New York Daily News,* something previously unheard of except in small town publications. It was the first time the tournament played to a sellout crowd. A chemistry seemed to happen at that tournament that spurred promotional activity in the sport.
4. First Women's Basketball Game in Madison Square Garden, February 22, 1975—The largest crowd ever to watch a women's basketball event, 11,000 plus, was on hand as the sport made its first appearance in a big-city major arena. The closely contested game between Immaculata and Queens proved that women could play their own exciting brand of basketball. Back then, the game in the Garden was considered unique, a happening. Today, an appearance in the Garden is just another whistle stop on the schedule of many teams.
5. 1974 Pre-Season Publicity—For the first time, national publications paid attention to the women in pre-season coverage.
6. Title IX of the Education Amendment Act, 1972—This law, prohibiting sexual discrimination in intercollegiate athletics at federally funded schools, gave women's sports the impetus to head for the big time. But many colleges were already making long-range plans in that direction. Title IX's greatest effect was in the high school programs, which now send freshmen into college programs each year with talent that is better than that found in the previous class.

7. Women's Basketball Becomes an Olympic Event, 1976—The U.S. won a silver medal. This event stirred the imagination of many female high school and college players who had one goal for the last four years—to make the U.S. team that was to compete in Moscow in 1980.
8. First Women's Weekly Top 20 Ratings, 1976—Commissioned by executive sports editor Jay Searcy, of the *Philadelphia Inquirer*, the poll's greatest asset was the communication it created around the country. Until that time, most information was by word of mouth. Now it was possible to learn how teams were doing each week. Two years later, the Associated Press began carrying the poll on its national wire.
9. The Women's Professional Basketball League Gets Off the Ground, 1978—The first women's pro league still has to prove it is here to stay. Several attempts to form a pro league in the past never got off the drawing board. By the 1978-79 season, the WBL was able to play a full schedule, all the way to a league championship.
10. AIAW Championship Is Nationally Televised, 1979—NBC televised the entire game on its show *Sportsworld*. The contest between Old Dominion and Louisiana Tech was competitive and brought the sport into homes where it had never before received exposure.
11. National Tournament Bracket Improved, 1980—The post-season field was enlarged to include 24 teams instead of the standard 16, as in the past decade. The traditional 16-team automatic qualifying method—through first or second in the region—was still in effect. But for the first time, eight more teams were selected as at-large entries, based on their in-season competition. Previously, a team that finished second in a region could only qualify if its region had a strong finish in the national tournament the previous year.
12. AIAW Allows Athletic Scholarships—This development was interrelated with Title IX. By allowing women to receive college scholarships for sports proficiency, the AIAW set the stage for the eventual swing to domination by large state-supported institutions over smaller ones.
13. Growth of Well-Run Camps and Clinics—The effect of this has been to provide much better coaching styles and better players throughout the decade.

14. AIAW's Rapid Membership Growth—In a four-year period, the AIAW has grown from 0 to more than 900 schools, giving it a membership that is larger than that of the NCAA. The effect was to eventually split the organization into Divisions I, II, and III for sports competition beginning in 1979-80.
15. Ed Jaworski's Involvement—Who is Ed Jaworski? If not for the former sports information director at Queen's College, many of these other developments would have taken much longer to come to pass. It was his work at the national tournament at Queens that helped spur the media interest that developed from this tournament. Also, to give special credit, without his knowledge of the early years, this list could not have been compiled.

PLAYERS

1. Theresa Shank Grentz—At 5-11, basketball's first "big woman" led Immaculata College, a tiny suburban Philadelphia women's college, to the first three national titles. She is now coach of Rutgers, which ended last season in the nation's top 10.
2. Lusia Harris Stewart—The 6-3 center of Delta State came on the scene after Grentz' graduation, and led the Lady Statesmen to the next three AIAW titles. She also scored the first field goal in Olympic competition, when she put two points in for the U.S. in the opening game in Montreal.
3. Carol Blazejowski—The former Montclair State All-America forward lit up the Madison Square Garden scoreboard in 1977 when she totaled 52 points, a record for the new Garden. She continued to rewrite scoring records throughout her senior year, when she led the Swans to third place in the AIAW Tournament. "The Blaze" was expected to be one of the stars of the Moscow Olympics.
4. Debbie Mason—At Queens College, she made the Knights a national contender. She was also one of the first of the flashy guards, enthralling the New York media with her spectacular style.
5. Nancy Lieberman—When the red-haired native of Far Rockaway, N.Y., takes the court for Old Dominion, she turns the arena into her own asphalt playground. She led the Monarchs to the national title in 1979, was the youngest

12
14

Nancy Lieberman made the U.S. Olympic team as a high school senior.
Old Dominion

Carol Blazejowski scored 52 points at Madison Square Garden.
Eileen Miller

member of the 1976 Olympic squad as a high school senior, and was expected to show her talent in Moscow. Lieberman was also the first player to be highly recruited, and she received offers of scholarships from 200 colleges.

6. Ann Meyers—One of the best team players around. At UCLA, Meyers was the nation's only four-time All-America. The sister of Milwaukee Bucks' forward Dave Meyers, she led the Bruins to the national title in her senior year, in 1978. She was a member of the U.S. Olympic squad in Montreal. And she became the first women to sign an NBA player contract when she inked with the Indiana Pacers. She was cut after three days and signed to play with the New Jersey Gems in the Women's Professional Basketball League.
7. Marianne Crawford Stanley—Stanley played her basketball at Immaculata, where she helped lead the Macs to two national titles with a style that was the women's version of the Philadelphia guard. She was on the first All-America team ever selected. In her two other seasons, Immaculata finished second to Delta State. In 1979, she became the first woman to win a national championship as a player and coach when she guided Old Dominion to the crown.
8. Inge Nissen—This 6–5 native of Denmark would be a star in any era. The Old Dominion center is devastating on the inside, and leads the nation in blocked shots. She would undoubtedly make the U.S. Olympic squad, but she has not been in the country long enough to satisfy the residency requirement.
9. Nancy Dunkel—A member of the U.S. Olympic squad in 1976, she played center with a certain style and grace that drew attention during her years at Cal. State Fullerton. She led the team to three national tournament appearances and coached the squad for two years after Billie Moore left for UCLA.
10. Sue Rojcewicz—A member of the U.S. squad in the 1976 Olympics, she starred at Southern Connecticut, where the Owls appeared in national tournaments all through her career. She is now assistant coach to Dotty McCrea at Stanford.
11. Debbie Brock—At 4–10, she is one of the tiniest guards who has ever played the game, but she has never let her size be a handicap. She was on Delta State's three national champion-

ship teams, and when Lucy Harris was bottled on the inside, Brock would come through with a deadly outside shot. She was also an All-America in her senior year.

12. Lynette Woodward—This University of Kansas star is just starting to realize her potential, but already can be listed as one of the great ones. She has a move to the inside that resembles Julius Erving's. She helped lead the U.S. to the gold medal in the World Games in 1979, with victories over Russia and Cuba.

COACHES

1. Cathy Rush, Immaculata—On and off the court, the wife of NBA official Ed Rush has been an innovator. During her career, her teams won three national titles, and finished second twice and fourth once. Through her efforts, women's basketball received the promotional lift it needed as she helped bring major industrial involvement to the sport. Retired, she now runs a series of camps and clinics throughout the country.
2. Lucille Kyvallos, Queens College—Times have changed, power has shifted, but Kyvallos' teams are still in the national picture. An innovator, she had Cathy Rush as a student at West Chester. The trademark of her teams has been their running style.
3. Billie Moore, UCLA—Success has been a constant in her career. Her Fullerton teams have made several national tournament appearances. She has won two national titles—with Fullerton in the second National Invitation Tournament before AIAW was formed, and with UCLA in 1978. She coached the U.S. Olympic team at Moscow.
4. Louise O'Neal, Southern Connecticut—Her teams made appearances in every National Invitation and AIAW tournament during her career. A solid teacher, she later coached at Yale, and is now head of the women's program at Dartmouth.
5. Sue Gunter, Stephen F. Austin—When coaches want to learn the 1-3-1 defense, they usually put in a call to Nacogdoches, Texas, to Gunter. Despite the swing of domination in the sport, Gunter's teams have remained successful. She was named coach of the U.S. Olympic squad in Moscow.

6. Dean Weese, Wayland Baptist—This gentleman enjoyed unusual success at a school located in a tiny Texas prairie town. His teams finished third and fourth in the national tournament. He is now coaching the Dallas entry in the women's pro league.
7. Margaret Wade, Delta State—Reviving a program that was dormant for 40 years, until 1973, her squads went on to become national powers, and won three national titles. The prestigious Wade Award, which goes to the outstanding junior or senior in the country, is named in her honor.
8. Carol Eckman, West Chester—Now at Lock Haven, this individual may be the true founder of the modern era. At West Chester, her teams were excellent, and she initiated the first National Invitation Tournament for college teams only. Coincidentally, her team won the first title.
9. Fran Schaafsma, Long Beach State—Until she retired from coaching, in 1979, her career spanned both eras of the sport. She was there in the beginning as one of the founders of AIAW, and later went on to have several of her squads in post-season play. She remains women's athletic director at the California school.
10. Judy Akers, Kansas State—Now retired, Akers' squads have always amazed the experts in Midwest basketball. Several times, she brought teams that had losing records at midseason, because of player injuries, back into a national tournament berth.
11. Maureen Wendelken, Montclair State—A coach whose teams seem to do it with mirrors. She managed to take a squad with a prolific scorer, Carol Blazejowski, and a bunch of supporting players and turn it into a national contender by weaving the two together. In 1979, with Blazejowski gone, Montclair State continued to give the top powers problems, and many attribute that to Wendelken's coaching.
12. Marynell Meadors, Tennessee Tech—Though it's been several years since her team has made a national tournament appearance, her squads have always been trouble for opponents during both the early and latter part of the decade.
13. Pat Head, Tennessee—Her forte has been her ability to attract talented players, some of whom are so inspired by her ability that they have transferred from other colleges to play for her. Her teams have never won *the* Game, but in the last

four years they have made three national tournament appearances and have reached the final four twice. She coached the silver-medal Pan-American team in 1979 and was named assistant coach for Moscow.

14. Fern Gardner, Utah—Though her teams have never been able to break through nationally in post-season play, she must be given credit for consistency in producing players and teams at Utah and Utah State that have always been in the regional title picture at season's end.

VIII

What's In A Name?

Stan Isaacs' Alphabetical Hall of Fame

When it comes to compiling lists, Stan Isaacs rushes in where other people fear to tread. A legend in his time for his chocolate ice-cream ratings, Isaacs graced the first *Book of Sports Lists* with his all-time listing of sports uniform numbers. Now he's here with an all-time, across-all-sports, alphabetical Hall of Fame list. His findings are personal and arbitrary, and he brooks no argument, though he admits to a bias that comes from (a) being a New Yorker and (b) growing up in the 1940s.

He names three for each letter, saying that the Rs are the strongest and claiming that he reached his finest hour by not being defeated by the Xs.

A—Muhammad Ali, Henry Aaron, Eddie Arcaro
B—Roger Bannister, Don Budge, Jimmy Brown
C—Roberto Clemente, Ty Cobb, Bob Cousy
D—Joe DiMaggio, Jack Dempsey, Babe Didrikson
E—Chrissie Evert-Lloyd, Julius Erving, Phil Esposito
F—Whitey Ford, Bob Feller, Dick Fosbury
G—Pancho Gonzales, Red Grange, Lou Gehrig

The world knew him as heavyweight boxing champion Joe Louis, but he hit hard on the golf course, too.

UPI

H—Gordie Howe, Sonja Henie, John Havlicek
I—Monte Irvin, Del Insko, Cecil Isbell
J—Jack Johnson, Bobby Jones, Hirsch Jacobs
K—Billie Jean King, Sandy Koufax, Kelso
L—Joe Louis, Kenesaw Mountain Landis, Rod Laver
M—Willie Mays, Stan Musial, Rocky Marciano
N—Jack Nicklaus, Paavo Nurmi, Bronko Nagurski
O—Al Oerter, Jesse Owens, Bobby Orr
P—Satchel Paige, Pelé, Pheidippides
Q—Adrian Quist, Quadrangle, Jack (baseball pitcher of the 1930s) Quinn
R—Babe Ruth, Jackie Robinson, Bill Russell
S—Casey Stengel, Willie Shoemaker, Harry M. Stevens
T—Jim Thorpe, Bill Tilden, Gene Tunney
U—Johnny Unitas, Bobby Ussery, Al Unser
V—Bill Veeck, Johnny Vander Meer, Ernie Vandeweghe
W—Helen Wills, John Wooden, Jerry West
X—Xochipilli (Mexican Indians' God of Sport), Xenophon (the Greek who invented the retreat tactic in warfare), Xalapa Crown (second in 1939 Santa Anita Derby)
Y—Carl Yastrzemski, Cy Young, Buddy Young
Z—Emil Zatopek, Tony Zale, Zev

20 Beautiful Names from the Ranks of Football

1. Christian K. Cagle
2. Aramis Dandoy
3. Atherton Phleger
4. Buzz Borries
5. Buzz Buivid
6. Banks McFadden
7. Father Lumpkin
8. Mad Dog O'Billovich
9. Proverb Jacobs
10. Viscount Francis
11. Wylie Fox
12. J. Bourbon Bondurant
13. Swinton Aldrich
14. Pesky Sprott
15. Lud Frentrup
16. Cloyce Box
17. Snorter Luster
18. Peahead Walker
19. Potsy Clarke
20. Greasy Neale

Kevin Demarrais' All-Ivy League Tweedy Name Team

Ivy League has an image of Brooks Brothers tweed jackets, prep school diplomas, club ties, a pipe in the mouth, and a fancy name.

Al Oerter won four Olympic gold medals in the discus.

UPI

Kevin Demarrais, veteran Sports Information Director at Columbia University, therefore presents his All-Ivy League Tweedy Name Team.

OFFENSE

End—Lauson Cashdollar, Princeton; Reginald Matson, Columbia
Tackle—Clark Wooley, Princeton; Hamilton McGregor, Columbia
Guard—Charles F. Eaton III, Harvard; Barton Blanchard, Columbia
Center—Roland Worthington, Columbia
Quarterback—Burke St. John, Harvard
Running Back—L. Scott Harshbarger, Harvard; Cabot Knowlton, Penn; Cosmo Iacavazzi, Princeton ("All right," says Demarrais, "I agree he shouldn't be there, but he had one of the all-time great names.")

DEFENSE

End—Maurice Snavely, Columbia; Duncan McCrann, Harvard
Tackle—S. Woodrow Sponaugle, Cornell; Perry Wickstrom, Yale
Middle Guard—Remington Ball, Princeton
Linebacker—Justin Harrington, Harvard; Spencer Ramsey, Columbia
Defensive back—Fairfax Hackley III, Dartmouth; R. Parker Crowell, Brown; E. Winters Mabry, Dartmouth; Brewster Loud, Princeton
Kicker—S. Scott Morrison, Princeton
Coach—Jordan Olivar, Yale

Michael Kunstler's 17 Jurisprudence All-Stars

Michael J. Kunstler presents a varied brief. He is a lawyer, was a longtime New York Giant baseball fan—his grandfather, Dr. M. Joseph Mandelbaum, was Christy Mathewson's eye, nose, and throat specialist—and has been associated with Frederick A. Johnson, the attorney who made the sporting and legal pages as Danny Gardella's attorney in his Mexican League case against

Jim Thorpe, voted the greatest athlete of the first half of the twentieth century, appears at the unveiling of a bust of Will Rogers in 1936.
UPI

Johnny Bench: Law and order at the plate.

Malcolm Emmons

organized baseball. Mr. Kunstler, whose brother William is the activist lawyer, ran on the Democratic ticket for the New York State Senate in the 36th district in 1978 and is still a mister.

1. Bench, Johnny Lee
2. Blackstone, Robert J.
3. Bond, Walter Franklin
4. Brief, Anthony Vincent
5. Case, George Washington
6. Crooks, John Charles
7. Frisk, John Emil
8. Gamble, Oscar Charles
9. Heist, Alfred Michael
10. Held, Woodson George
11. Judge, Joseph Ignatius
12. Just, Joseph Erwin
13. Law, Vernon Sanders
14. Loan, William Joseph
15. Outlaw, James Paulus
16. Spies, Henry
17. Warden, Jonathan Edgar

8 Baseball Players in Major League History with 13 Letters in Their Last Names

1. Gene DeMontreville
2. Lee DeMontreville
3. Al Hollingsworth
4. Bonnie Hollingsworth
5. Austin Knickerbocker
6. Billy Knickerbocker
7. Ken Raffensberger
8. Ossee Schreckengost

13 Sports Personalities Better Known as "Dutch" Than by Their Real First Names

1. Dutch Dotterer, baseball (Henry John)
2. Dutch Dehnert, basketball (Henry)
3. Dutch Hoefer, basketball (Charles)
4. Dutch Hiller, hockey (Carl Wilbert)
5. Dutch Reibel, hockey (Earl)
6. Dutch Garfinkel, basketball (Jack)
7. Dutch Feutsch, basketball (Herman)
8. Dutch Leonard, baseball (Emil John)
9. Dutch Leonard, baseball (Hubert Benjamin)
10. Dutch Meyer, football (Leo)
11. Dutch Clack, football (Earl)
12. Dutch Lancaster, basketball (Jim)
13. Dutch Harrison, golf (E. J.)

EDITORS' NOTE: Norm Van Brocklin, Cornelius Warmerdam, and Ronald Reagan, sports broadcaster-turned-movie actor-turned-politician, were also known as "Dutch," but were more commonly

known by their given names; Dutch Lancaster is the brother of movie star Burt Lancaster.

Bill O'Donnell's 10 Favorite Baseball Nicknames

Bill O'Donnell, who admits to having no nickname, broadcasts the games of the Baltimore Orioles.

1. Bananas (Zeke Bonura)
2. Boog (John Powell)
3. Twinkletoes (George Selkirk)
4. Motormouth (Paul Blair)
5. Blade (Mark Belanger)
6. Snuffy (George Stirnweiss)
7. Cakes (Jim Palmer)
8. Fat Freddie (Fred Fitzsimmons)
9. Gray Fox (Jim Northrup)
10. Snake (Pat Dobson)

Roy Blount, Jr.'s 15 Major Sports Juniors

Roy Blount, Jr., is a freelance writer and the author of a book about the Pittsburgh Steelers, *About Three Bricks Shy of a Load* (Little Brown). He majored in English at Vanderbilt and Harvard and has written for *Sports Illustrated,* the *New Yorker* and the *New York Times.* He has been a Junior since birth, and a Junior-watcher ever since.

1. Cassius Marcellus Clay, Jr. (Muhammad Ali)
2. Willie Howard Mays, Jr.
3. Giuseppe Paolo (Joseph Paul) DiMaggio, Jr.
4. Harry Lillis "Bing" Crosby, Jr.
5. Philip Henry Niekro, Jr.
6. Vida Blue, Jr.
7. Dock Phillip Ellis, Jr.
8. John McEnroe, Jr.
9. Angel Cordero, Jr.
10. Laffit Pincay, Jr.
11. Kyle Rote, Jr.

Original Celtic Dutch Dehnert created the pivot play.

Dutch Dehnert Collection

John McEnroe, Jr., had a meteoric rise to center court.

UPI

12. Louis Boudreau, Jr.
13. Lucius Benjamin (Luke) Appling, Jr.
14. James William (Junior) Gilliam, Jr.
15. Junior Johnson (The Last American Hero)

Adds Blount, Jr.: "Bing Crosby is included not as a singer, but as a former owner of the Pittsburgh Pirates. Some of the baseball Juniors aren't identified as such in the *Baseball Encyclopedia,* which is very haphazard about Juniors."

Willie Howard Mays, Jr., broke in as a New York Giant at the Polo Grounds.

UPI

Bobby Hull's speed, fast shot, goal-scoring instincts, and strength made him the perfect player.

Barton Silverman

IX

Winter Wonderland

Hugh Delano's Potpourri of Hockey, from Great Names, Past and Present, to Cigar Smokers, to Best Dressed, to Haircuts, to Meanies, to Intellectuals, to . . .

Hugh Delano, of the *New York Post,* has been on the hockey beat for the past dozen years and recalls seeing his first hockey game in 1947 ("Turk Broda and Chuck Rayner battled to a 2-2 tie," he says).

21 GREATEST NICKNAMES

1. Bob "Battleship" Kelly
2. John "Pie Face" McKenzie
3. Dave "The Hammer" Schultz
4. Bryan "Bugsy" Watson
5. Andre "Moose" Dupont
6. Bryan "Soupy" Campbell
7. Jerry "King Kong" Korab
8. Don "Big Bird" Saleski
9. Yvan "The Road Runner" Cournoyer
10. Mike "Shaky" Walton
11. Frank "Never" Beaton
12. Mike "Worm" Veisor

13. Bill "Cowboy" Flett
14. Gary "The Cobra" Simmons
15. Dale "Goat" Rolfe
16. Bob "Hound" Kelly
17. Reggie "Cement Head" Fleming
18. Glen "Slats" Sather
19. Ed "Box Car" Hospodar
20. Bernie "Boom Boom" Geoffrion
21. George "Punch" Imlach

35 GREAT NAMES FROM YESTERYEAR

1. Killer Kaleta
2. Bun Cook
3. Flash Hollett
4. Baldy Cotton
5. Cyclone Taylor
6. Crash Cushenan
7. Mush March
8. Nipper O'Hearn
9. Pud Glass
10. Mud Bruneteau
11. Yip Foster
12. Bronco Horvath
13. Bones Raleigh
14. Knobby Warwick
15. Shrimp Worters
16. Bullet Joe Simpson
17. Wild Bill Ezinicki
18. Sugar Jim Henry
19. Busher Jackson
20. Buzz Boll
21. Ivan "The Terrible" Irwin
22. Mel "Sudden Death" Hill
23. Ching Johnson
24. Camille "The Eel" Henry
25. Johnny "Black Cat" Gagnon
26. Eddie "Clear the Track" Shack
27. Black Jack Stewart
28. Harry "Apple Cheeks" Lumley
29. Turk Broda
30. Taffy Abel
31. Zellio Toppazini

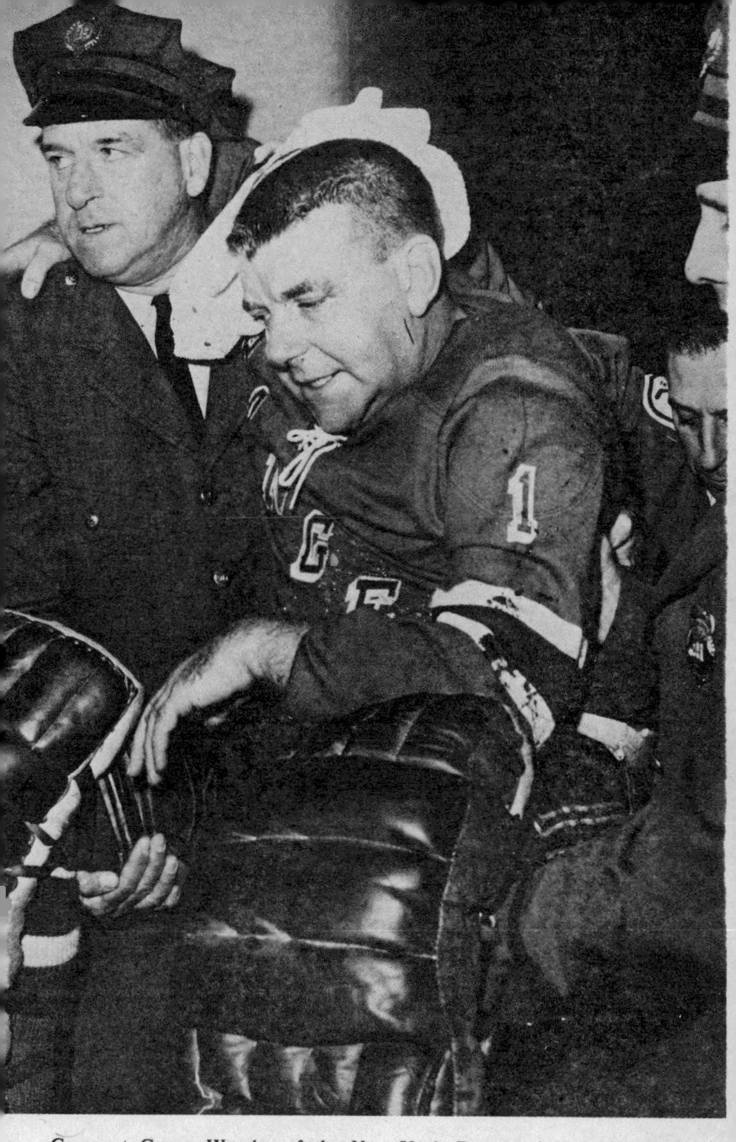

Crew-cut Gump Worsley of the New York Rangers is helped off the Madison Square Garden ice after sustaining a head cut in a 1963 game against the Montreal Canadiens.

UPI

32. Odie Lowe
33. Frankie "Mr. Zero" Brimsek
34. Sprague Cleghorn
35. Gump Worsley

11 MOST FASCINATING NAMES

Says Delano: "The Buffalo Sabres drafted a left wing named Morris Titanic in 1973. When he fell short of their expectations and was demoted to the minor leagues, a one-paragraph story in the sports pages was headlined 'Titanic Goes Down Again.' "

1. Morris Titanic
2. Bart Crashley
3. Butch Deadmarsh
4. John "Butch" Baby
5. Jimmy Boo
6. Ted Bulley
7. Mal Zinger
8. Jim Moxey
9. Kelly Greenbank
10. Brent Meeke
11. Darryl Sly

THE RAINBOW ALL-STARS

Goalie—Andy Brown
Defensemen—Ted Green, Bill White
Forwards—Brian Lavender, Terry Gray, Milt Black
Coach—Red Kelly

THE ALL-IN-THE-FAMILY TEAM

Goalies—Bill Smith, Gary Smith, Al Smith
Defensemen—Dallas Smith, Rick Smith, Gord Smith, Greg Smith
Forwards—Bobby Smith, Brad Smith, Derek Smith
Coach—Floyd Smith

THE ALL-PHYSICAL TEAM

Goalie—Don Head
Defensemen—Gregg Boddy, Gerry Hart, Randy Legge
Forward—John Flesch
Coach—Toe Blake

6 GREATEST CIGAR SMOKERS

1. Mike Nykoluk
2. John Ferguson
3. Carol Vadnais
4. Tom Johnson
5. Alex Delvecchio
6. Johnny Bucyk

3 BEST-DRESSED COACHES

Says Delano: "No contest. Don Cherry is in a class by himself. He seldom wears the same outfit twice. He started the trend with the Boston Bruins and took it with him to the Colorado Rockies. Custom-tailored Edwardian-style three-piece suits with gold watch chains in his vest pockets and crushed velvet jackets are his favorites."

1. Don Cherry
2. Bernie "Boom Boom" Geoffrion
3. Pat Quinn

7 BEST-DRESSED PLAYERS

Says Delano: "Ron Stewart played 21 years in the NHL without ever being caught off the ice with a wrinkle in his trousers, shoes that didn't have a mirrorlike shine, or a necktie not knotted perfectly. He cared for his fashionable wardrobe as much as players care for their sticks and skates. He was so neat, he always took an iron with him on road trips."

1. Ron Stewart
2. Sheldon Kannegiesser
3. Jean Ratelle
4. Rod Gilbert
5. Vic Hadfield
6. Carol Vadnais
7. Guy Lafleur

2 LAST CREW CUTS

1. Pat Stapleton
2. Gump Worsley

1 DESIGNATED SPITTER

1. Rick Foley

Says Delano: "Rick Foley, a giant-sized Philadelphia Flyers' defenseman, once got into an argument with New York Rangers' general manager-coach Emile Francis. Foley skated to the Rangers' bench and spit for several minutes toward Francis. 'Foley spits like he plays hockey,' joked Francis. 'He never hit me once.' "

1 STRONGEST MAN

1. Tim Horton

Says Delano: "The late Tim Horton, a mild-mannered man, once amazed New York Rangers' teammates by picking up and moving a hotel soft-drink vending machine. He wore glasses off the ice and bore a slight resemblance to Clark Kent. His teammates nicknamed him Superman."

5 MOST INTELLECTUAL PLAYERS

1. Ken Dryden
2. Curt Bennett
3. Denis Potvin
4. Syl Apps
5. Gary Inness

Delano notes: "Goaltender Dryden graduated from Cornell University and retired from the Montreal Canadiens to pursue his law career. It would not be surprising to see him follow former pro basketball star Bill Bradley into politics."

9 PLAYERS TO AVOID IN A FIGHT

1. Nick Fotiu
2. Curt Bennett
3. Dan Maloney
4. Bob Nystrom
5. Garry Howatt
6. Barry Beck
7. Terry O'Reilly
8. Paul Holmgren
9. Larry Robinson

ALL-MEANIE TEAM

Goalie—Bill Smith
Defensemen—Steve Durbano, Bryan "Bugsy" Watson
Forwards—Dave Schultz, Dave "Tiger" Williams, Nick Fotiu
Coach—John Ferguson

7 HARDEST SHOTS

1. Bobby Hull
2. Rick MacLeish
3. Dennis Hull
4. Larry Sacharuk
5. Barry Beck
6. Rick Martin
7. Jacques Lemaire

3 SLICKEST PLAYMAKERS

1. Jean Ratelle
2. Bobby Clarke
3. Stan Mikita

2 BEST DEFENSIVE FORWARDS

1. Bob Gainey
2. Don Marcotte

4 BEST FACE-OFF MEN

1. Derek Sanderson
2. Pete Stemkowski
3. Doug Jarvis
4. Phil Esposito

4 BEST PENALTY KILLERS

1. Bobby Clarke
2. Walt Tkaczuk
3. Eddie Westfall
4. Don Luce

3 BEST SKATERS

1. Bobby Orr
2. Guy Lefleur
3. Bobby Hull

3 MOST DANGEROUS SCORING THREATS

1. Phil Esposito
2. Guy Lafleur
3. Mike Bossy

5 BEST ALL-AROUND DEFENSEMEN

1. Bobby Orr
2. Denis Potvin
3. Brad Park
4. Larry Robinson
5. Borje Salming

2 BEST DEFENSIVE DEFENSEMEN

1. Bill White
2. Serge Savard

3 BEST ALL-AROUND PLAYERS

1. Bobby Orr
2. Bobby Clarke
3. Bryan Trottier

2 BEST BREAKAWAY THREATS

1. Yvan Cournoyer
2. Guy Lafleur

3 FASTEST SKATERS

1. Gene Carr
2. Guy Lafleur
3. Yvan Cournoyer

5 QUICKEST ONE-ON-ONE MOVES

1. Bobby Orr
2. Guy Lafleur
3. Gilbert Perreault
4. Marcel Dionne
5. Rick Middleton

3 BEST GOALTENDERS

1. Bernie Parent
2. Tony Esposito
3. Ken Dryden

2 BEST BIG-GAME GOALTENDERS

1. Gerry Cheevers
2. Tony Esposito

1 MOST DETERMINED GOALTENDER

1. Eddie Giacomin

Delano adds: "Giacomin's hand was sliced open by Bobby Hull's skate in the 1971 playoffs. Eddie refused to leave the game to have the wound closed with stitches. He told New York Rangers' trainer Frank Paice to put a bandage on the painfully deep gash. With his glove filled with blood, Giacomin finished the game, and the Rangers beat Chicago in overtime. It was typical of Giacomin. He was badly burned in a kitchen fire when he was a teenager and told he would never play hockey again. Scouts told him he'd never make it as an NHL goalie, but, after spending five years in the minor leagues, he went on to become an NHL all-star."

4 SMARTEST COACHES

1. Scotty Bowman
2. Fred Shero
3. Al Arbour
4. Don Cherry

1 HARDEST-WORKING TEAM EXECUTIVE

1. Emile "The Cat" Francis

1 MOST INTENSE COMPETITOR

1. Keith Magnuson

Says Delano: "The Chicago Black Hawks' Keith Magnuson psyched himself up so much before games that he would burst on ice for pre-game warmups and speed-skate around the rink while teammates skated in leisurely circles. It was the only way the red-haired defenseman could release his pent-up energy."

The Canadiens' Ken Dryden, a lawyer, used his head at all times.

UPI

Bobby Orr as a 15-year-old with Oshawa.

Oshawa Times

6 BIGGEST FLAKES

1. Gilles Gratton
2. Jim Pettie
3. Steve Durbano
4. Mike "Shaky" Walton
5. Derek Sanderson
6. Dunc Wilson

Adds Delano: "Boston Bruins' and New York Rangers' goalie Jim Pettie once was caught running through the corridor of a hotel without his clothes on. Rangers' goalie Gilles Gratton once streaked across the ice with nothing on but his skates. He believed he had been reincarnated after being a soldier in the Spanish Inquisition. "You have to be crazy to be a goaltender, anyway,' he said."

2 GREATEST COMICS

1. Pete Stemkowski
2. Vic Hadfield

Delano notes: "Detroit Red Wings' coach Ned Harkness, a former Cornell coach, caught Pete Stemkowski leading the team in a mock Cornell rah-rah cheer at practice. When he ordered Stemkowski to get his hair cut, Stemkowski did so, but he sent an envelope filled with his trimmings to Harkness. He was immediately traded to the New York Rangers, where he kept his teammates in stitches with zany antics, jokes, one-liners, and realistic imitations of Hollywood stars and disc jockeys. Vic Hadfield used to hide teammates' false teeth and dental bridgework in the dressing room after games or practice."

6 MOST HUSTLING PLAYERS

1. Bobby Clarke
2. Ron Harris
3. Bruce MacGregor
4. Bob "Hound" Kelly
5. Joe Watson
6. Ted Irvine

1 BEST CORNERMAN

1. Wayne Cashman

1 TOUGHEST MAN IN FRONT OF THE NET

1. Gary Dornhoefer

1 MOST GENTLEMANLY PLAYER

1. Jean Ratelle

4 MOST INJURY-PRONE PLAYERS

1. Keith Magnuson
2. Jim Schoenfeld
3. Gary Doak
4. Ab DeMarco

1 LEAST INJURY-PRONE PLAYER

1. Garry Unger—He hasn't missed a game in 12 years.

1 MOST REMARKABLE PLAYER

1. Gordie Howe—Who else? He's in his fifties, a grandfather, and started playing in the 1940s, played through the 1950s, 1960s, and 1970s, and into the 1980s.

Ageless Gordie Howe was still playing in the NHL in his fifties.
Bruce Bennett

Art Devlin's 10 Greatest Ski Jumpers

As a nine-year-old, Art Devlin watched the 1932 Winter Olympic Games from a high branch on a tree in his hometown, in Lake Placid, New York. In 1980, he was an announcer for ABC-TV at the Winter Olympics in Lake Placid. In between, he achieved a distinguished record as a world-class skier and a three-time Olympian. On his list, you won't find the name of the late Torger Tokle, a native of Norway who came to the United States in 1939 and won 42 of 48 meets before he joined the U.S. Army. He never made it to the Olympics—he was killed in 1945 in action as a ski trooper with the 10th Mountain Division in Italy. "I didn't include Torger because he didn't get to compete internationally," explains Devlin.

1. Birger Ruud, Norway
2. Reider Andersen, Norway
3. Sigmund Ruud, Norway
4. Sepp Bradel, Austria
5. Hans Georg Aschenbach, East Germany
6. Bjourn Wirkola, Norway
7. Walter Steiner, Switzerland
8. Yukio Kasaya, Japan
9. Antii Hyvarinen, Finland
10. Toni Innauer, Austria

Devlin notes: "Birger Ruud was the most remarkable of all. Consider that he achieved a double never equalled, by winning both a Nordic and an Alpine event in the 1936 Olympics. Not only did he successfully defend the jumping gold he had won four years earlier, but Ruud also finished first in the downhill. Then, following a 12-year gap between Olympics, due to World War II, he earned a silver medal in jumping in 1948—16 years after he'd won his first gold."

Freestyle America's 10 Greatest Combined Freestyle Skiers of All Time

Freestyle America is a skiing organization formed by Tracey Kasel and twin brothers Peter and Yetta Rushford. Having skied all of their lives, the three organized and perform the best skiing entertainment show throughout the world, and have competed successfully themselves as professional freestyle skiers. They work with ski-industry manufacturers on a promotional and sales level

Art Devlin jumps in Germany in 1952.

Art Devlin Collection

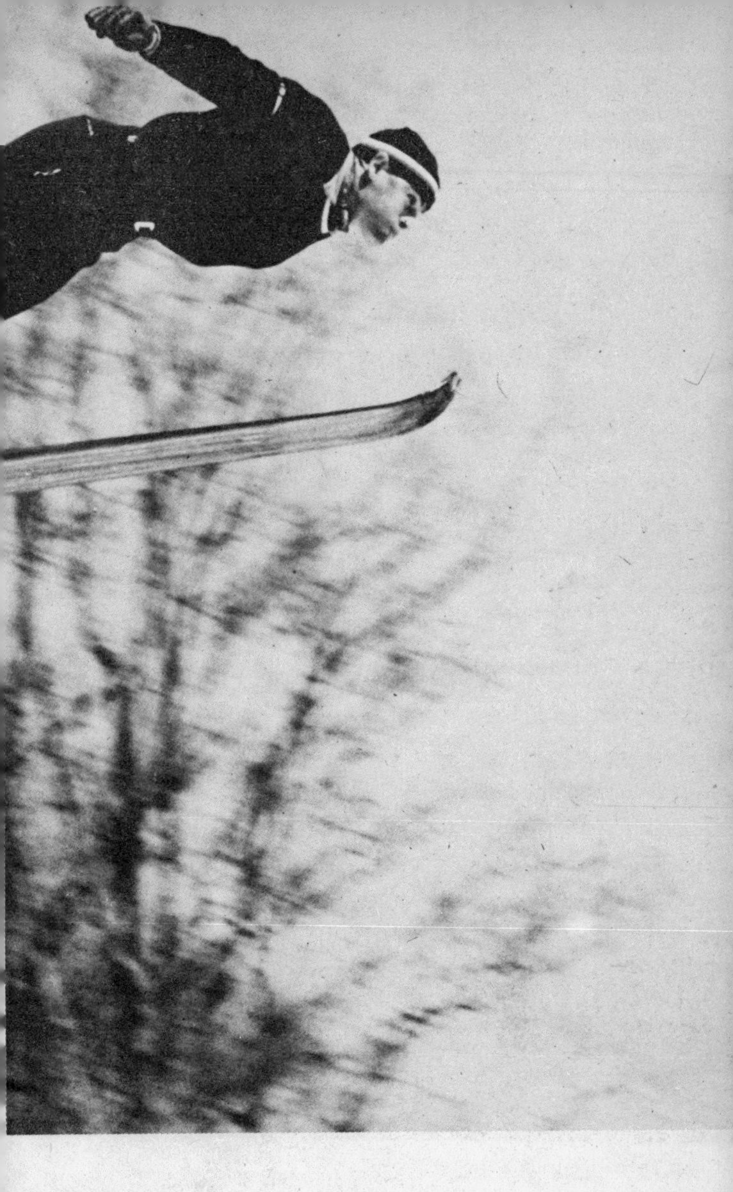

and also have an extensive background in leading freestyle programs and instruction. The members of Freestyle America are not included in this list.

1. John Eaves
2. Greg Athans
3. Wayne Wong
4. Scott Brooksbank
5. Bob Salerno
6. Mark Stiegemeier
7. Steve Rezendes
8. Rick Bowie
9. Bruce Bolesky
10. Suzy Chaffee

Bob Perry's 10 Greatest Skiing Photographers

Bob Perry got his introduction to cold-weather photography by doing Arctic shooting for Western Electric, where he is now Audio-Visual Supervisor for Motion Pictures. Twenty years ago, he embarked on a winter weekend career as ski photographer at the Killington (Vt.) Ski Resort. He can ski backwards, a must for all good ski photographers who want to capture the downhill schussboomers. He has produced and photographed four award-winning films. Notes Perry, who refused to include himself on the list: "There are other good ones, I'm sure, but the ones I've picked are those whose work I've seen and admired for many years. I've listed them alphabetically."

1. Hanson Carroll
2. Norm Clasen
3. Fred Lindholm
4. Peter Miller
5. Del Mulkey
6. Scott Nelson
7. Peter Runyon
8. Hubert Schriebl
9. Clyde Smith
10. Barry Stott

Lou Goldstein's 10 Greatest Barrel Jumpers

The sport of barrel jumping on ice skates, born in Holland centuries ago, has long been a staple along with borscht, blintzes, and Lou Goldstein at Grossinger's, the Catskill Mountain resort in New York State. Goldstein, whose Simon Sez routine has made him the most popular figure at the hotel, and a television personality as well, is Grossinger's Director of Daytime Entertainment and Athletic Activities. Since 1951, when former Olympic speed-skating champion Irv Jaffee instituted the World Barrel-Jumping

This is one of Bob Perry's favorites from his own collection, shot at Killington in Vermont.

Bob Perry

Barrel jumping at Grossinger's.

Grossinger's

Championships, Goldstein has watched the jumpers from up front. The name of the Grossinger competition has changed over the years to the North American Championships in 1977 to the International Team Barrel-Jumping Championships in 1979, when NBC televised the action.

1. Ken LeBel—He jumped over 17 barrels for a world record in 1965. So did Jacques Favero in the Canadian championships, but LeBel had a 28-foot, 7½-inch jump to Favero's 28-footer.
2. Leo LeBel—Older brother of Ken.
3. Terry Browne—The Flying Fireman from Detroit who was the first champion, in 1951.
4. James Papreck—He set a world record of 29-4½ over 16 barrels. Notes Goldstein: "They changed the rules for take-off distance. Usually the jumper must take off from 30 inches or less before the first barrel. ABC, which was televising the event, wanted a new record, and Irv Jaffee changed the take-off distance to 42 inches."
5. Rowland Sylvester—1973 world champion.
6. Roger Wood—1972 world champion.
7. Richard Widmark—Not the actor. He was an outstanding speedskater from Northbrook, Ill.
8. Jacques Favero
9. Gilles LeClerc—A Canadian record-holder, he did 28–3 over 16 barrels.
10. Yvon Jolin Jr.—Winner of the 1979 Grossinger competition.

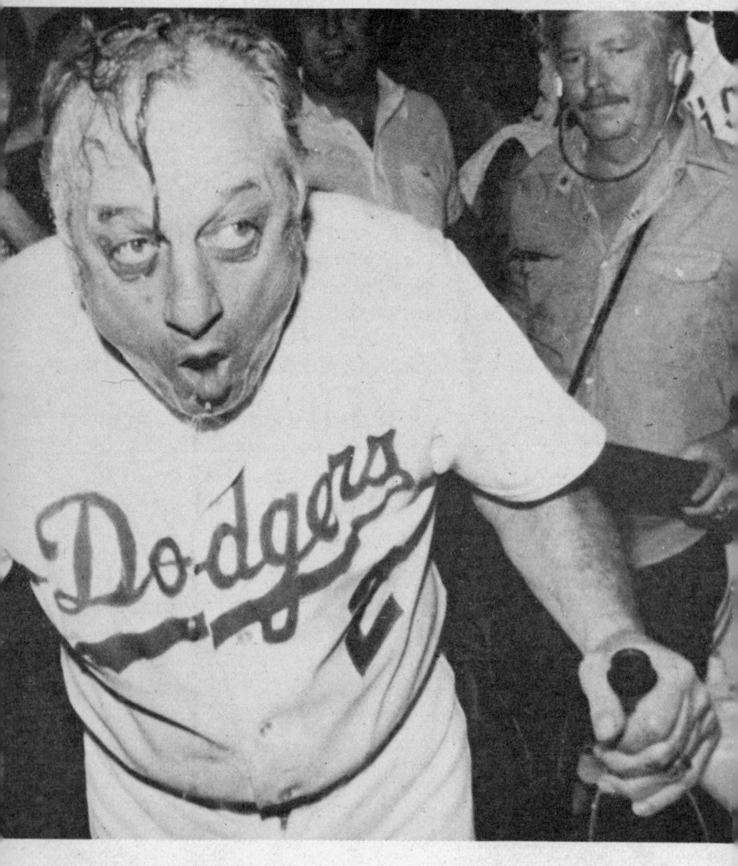

Champagne doesn't usually accompany clubhouse food unless there's a title celebration, such as this one at which Tom Lasorda took the bubbly after his Dodgers won the National League West crown in 1978.

UPI

X

Galloping Gourmets

Tom Lasorda's Ratings of Food in National League Clubhouses

Dodger manager Tom Lasorda knows food. His family runs a restaurant in suburban Philadelphia, and he has dined in restaurants and clubhouses from Canada to Puerto Rico. "I haven't run into a bad meal yet," Lasorda says. "I postpone a few, but I never miss any." Each major league clubhouse attendant provides a post-game meal for the team, and Lasorda agreed to rate the clubhouse spread for the *Los Angeles Times*. His top choices were awarded four stars (****), his bottom choices got one star (*).

1. Los Angeles (****)—"My office has got to be a four star. We always have egg rolls and pork sent over from a Chinese restaurant. Joe [a friend who works for a food company] brings bologna, pepperonis, burritos, and stuff like that for the office. A local deli sends hero sandwiches, and an Italian restaurant sends some stuff over sometimes when they feel generous."
2. New York (****)—"The reason it's good is his [clubhouse man's] mom cooks the food, and she's Italian. He has

rigatoni, meat loaf, ham and cheese, chicken, mostaccioli. The mostaccioli is delicious. That's probably the best meal on the road."

3. San Francisco (****)—"I like Murph [clubhouse man]. He has steak sandwiches, hamburger steaks, chicken, plus tomatoes and all the stuff that comes with it. It's probably as good as eating in a restaurant. He takes a special interest in the players."
4. Philadelphia (***)—"The guy has good stuff, but he never varies it. It's the same every time. But it's good. Polish sausage, hot dogs, cold cuts. His New Jersey-style sliced tomatoes are very good."
5. Chicago (***)—"Good. He goes more for quantity than quality. He feels if you put out a lot of food, no one complains. Even if he puts out only one thing, there'll be a lot of it."
6. St. Louis (***)—"He specializes in chicken. He puts out good-quality food."
7. Houston (***)—"The guy's good there. I think he's the only one in the league who has beer on tap. He's a Cuban fellow and a lot of times he delves a little more in spicy food."
8. Cincinnati (**)—"He has a nice room. He deals in a lot of chili. He cooks the meals right there. The guy gets a lower grade because he started locking the refrigerator before games."
9. Atlanta (**)—"Good. He's a chicken man, too. He tries to delve into southern hospitality. The hospitality is great, but the food isn't. He's got southern dishes, but there's nothing on the dish."
10. San Diego (*)—"Not that good. The only good thing is the eating room; it's separate from the clubhouse. The guy goes with the same pattern—skinny chickens. He must get chickens that are smuggled out of Tijuana."
11. Montreal (*)—"The worst in the business. He puts out chicken. I think the way they were killed was he starved them to death."
12. Pittsburgh (*)—"It's in a class with Montreal. The guy figures he's not gonna give you good food so he can make a profit. One day out of three or four he has something hot. I think he had a relative who was killed in a supermarket and he doesn't want to get it the same way, so he buys everything off the streets. Whatever he's serving, it's imitation."

Baseball Players' 10 Favorite Restaurants in New York

1. The Palm
2. The Stage Deli
3. Gallagher's Steak House
4. Mamma Leone's
5. Maxwell's Plum
6. Patsy's
7. Christo's
8. The English Pub
9. Tavern on the Green
10. Rusty's

The above list was prepared by Dick O'Connor, of the *Palo Alto Times,* who surveyed 60 major league players on their preferences in New York City.

Maury Allen's 10 Best and 10 Worst Free-Load Goodies in Baseball Press Boxes

As a baseball writer for the *New York Post* for almost 20 years, Maury Allen has sampled the "goodies" and "baddies" in every major league press box.

BEST

1. Crab cakes in Baltimore
2. Ice cream in Detroit
3. Cookies in Detroit
4. Dessert in Boston
5. Hot dogs in Milwaukee
6. Waitress in Minnesota
7. Hard cheese in Boston
8. Anything in Anaheim
9. Sundaes in Philadelphia
10. Ball girls in Philadelphia

WORST

1. Chop suey at Shea Stadium
2. Wrinkled lettuce in San Francisco
3. Burnt chicken at Yankee Stadium
4. Depressing atmosphere in Oakland
5. Paper plates in Montreal
6. Hot sauces in Houston
7. Crowds in Dodger Stadium press room
8. Guards in Atlanta
9. Stale cookies in Cincinnati
10. Burnt hamburgers in St. Louis

Captain Moss Bunker's 10 Favorite Fish

Capt. Moss Bunker is the former fishing editor of the late *Rudder* magazine, the first yachting magazine established in the United

States. He is fishing editor of *The Ensign,* official publication of the U.S. Power Squadrons, the 80,000-member national boating organization. Capt. Bunker likes not only to catch fish, but to eat them, as well. He has fished around the world and covered numerous big- and small-game tournaments, from the White Marlin Tournament in Bimini, Bahamas, to the U.S. Atlantic Tuna Tournament on Cape Cod, Mass. Here are his 10 favorite salt-water fish, not necessarily on the hook, but decidedly on the platter.

1. Strawberry grouper
2. King mackerel
3. Summer flounder
4. Albacore
5. Swordfish
6. Scup
7. Salmon
8. Bonita
9. Red snapper
10. Sardines (King Oscar)

XI

A Kick In The Grass

Temple Pouncey's Best Players, Best Americans, Biggest Flops, Nastiest, Sneakiest, Ugliest, Most Inspirational, Most Overrated, Most Underrated, Gunners, Best Shooters, Fastest, Best Goalkeepers, Flakiest, Best and Worst Places to Play, Most Poorly Run Franchises, and Cutest Teams in Soccer

Temple Pouncey, of the *Dallas Morning News,* has covered the North American Soccer League from its inception. He says: "Soccer stars are new to the North American public. We didn't grow up with them; they weren't on our TV sets and passed around as bubble-gum cards. To most people, they are just names, or, at best, faceless bodies known by their shirt numbers. These lists are designed to give some of the flavor and texture of the Anglo-Latino-Slavic NASL player. You still might not know as much about Ace Ntsoelengoe as you do about Pete Rose, but we must keep this in perspective."

BEST PLAYERS

1. Johan Cruyff
2. Ace Ntsoelengoe
3. Alan Ball
4. Franz Beckenbauer
5. Carlos Alberto

The Los Angeles Aztecs' Johan Cruyff, a native of Holland, was 1979 MVP in the North American Soccer League.

Los Angeles Aztecs

Notes Pouncey: "In just one year in this country, Cruyff proved he is the genuine article. And one Ace Ntsoelengoe is worth two 33-year-old former English internationals now playing on one leg."

BEST AMERICANS

1. Ricky Davis
2. Alan Mayer
3. Tony Bellinger
4. Perry Van Der Beck
5. Pat Fidelia

Notes Pouncey: "Being a good American soccer player, someone once said, is like being the best second baseman in Austria. Americans are usually good for public relations, meeting league requirements, and sitting on the bench. However, a few actually play regularly in the NASL, including Davis, who not only starts, but excels, for the glamorous Cosmos."

BIGGEST FLOPS

1. Peter Osgood
2. Geoff Hurst
3. Mirandinha
4. Johnny Giles
5. Andy Lochhead

Notes Pouncey: "The Philadelphia Fury paid Osgood $90,000 in 1978, for which the former English international forward repaid them with one goal—and benched himself for the final game. Hurst was fat and out of shape when he played for Seattle, 10 years after his 1966 World Cup glory days. Ex-Brazil World Cup star Mirandinha likewise managed just one goal for Tampa Bay, which dumped him to the Memphis Rogues. Giles, 35 at the time, was another reason the '78 Fury was a dismal failure. Another former English international, Lochhead, didn't keep the 1974 Denver Dynamos from scraping the bottom of the league—and going on to Minnesota to become the Kicks."

NASTIEST PLAYERS

1. Colin Waldron
2. John Rowlands
3. Steve Seargeant
4. Dave D'Errico
5. Bobby Thompson

Notes Pouncey: "These are people who would just as soon kick you as look at you. They would break your leg to give themselves a breather. Waldron was such a runaway winner that the others could not compare, although Rowlands was a strong second."

SNEAKIEST FOULERS

1. Vladislav Bogicevic
2. Alan Merrick
3. John Craven
4. Zeljko Tuksa
5. Paul Child

Notes Pouncey: "Bogicevic does not get caught often, but he has a knack for planting an elbow in an opponent's neck and skipping off Yugoslav-free. Merrick used his arms as well as anyone who ever played the game. Craven, Vancouver's defensive leader, committed only 13 fouls in the 1979 season, despite playing all 30 games. Who can believe that?"

UGLIEST PLAYERS

1. Jan Van Der Veen
2. Archie Roboostoff
3. Graham Day
4. Henry McCully
5. Bobby Smith

Notes Pouncey: "Van Der Veen is one of the reasons soccer teams don't have picture trading cards."

MOST INSPIRATIONAL

1. Alan Ball
2. Johan Cruyff
3. Alan Merrick
4. Jan Van Der Veen
5. Jim Steele

MOST OVERRATED

1. Shep Messing
2. Phil Parkes
3. Alan West
4. Mike England
5. Omar (El Indio) Gomez

Notes Pouncey: "Messing doesn't keep changing teams only because he can get more money. He did a better job of promoting himself than anybody else, so his name exceeds his talent. For all his honors, Parkes would not be leading the league in goaltending if he did not have Craven and the rest of the Vancouver defense in front of him."

MOST UNDERRATED

1. Mick Poole
2. Kai Haaskivi
3. David Irving
4. Wolfgang Rausch
5. Pat Fidelia

Made in America, the New York Cosmos' Ricky Davis leads the native-born in the NASL.

New York Cosmos

Notes Pouncey: "It takes years to build a name in soccer. You must play in the right city for the right team. NASL fans would love to see Poole play in front of a Vancouver-like defense. Then he wouldn't have to make so many flying, acrobatic saves."

GUNNERS OF THE WORLD

1. Karl-Heinz Granitza
2. Francisco Marinho
3. Giorgio Chinaglia
4. Jeff Bourne
5. Willi Lippens

Notes Pouncey: "Granitza will shoot anytime, from anywhere, as proved by his record 216 shots in 1979. Marinho's specialty is the solo run followed by the 30-yard bomb. Try getting any of these guys to pass the ball to you inside the 35-yard line."

BEST SHOOTERS

1. Neill Roberts
2. Wayne Hughes
3. Zequinha
4. Thomas Sjoberg
5. Oscar Fabbiani

Notes Pouncey: "Atlanta's Roberts was the NASL shooting champion in 1979, sinking 14 of his 46 shots, a .304 average. Hughes made seven out of seven from the penalty shot. Zequinha of Dallas scored every penalty and every shootout shot he was asked to take."

FASTEST

1. Elson Seale
2. Flemming Lund
3. Steve David
4. Seninho
5. Johan Cruyff

Notes Pouncey: "Seale is the league's most effective substitute. With 20 minutes left and his opponents wheezing, he comes in and begins sprinting down the wing. Dallas' Lund, who wears size 5½ shoes, is the most tireless runner of them all—and maybe the smartest. Cruyff makes the list on his sudden acceleration alone."

BEST GOALKEEPERS

1. Mick Poole
2. Paul Hammond
3. Alan Mayer
4. Phil Parkes
5. Bill Irwin

Notes Pouncey: "Poole and Mayer make the most spectacular saves. Hammond is the steadiest, and the best in the shootout. Irwin is reliable and tough, and Parkes is the most punishing and the most colorful—he blew kisses to the Cosmos' fans at Giants Stadium before the '79 Soccer Bowl."

FLAKIEST

1. Shep Messing
2. Steve David
3. Bobby Smith
4. George Best
5. Paul Cannell

Notes Pouncey: "If Messing hadn't clinched this one with his snakes, his *Viva* pose, and his autobiography, he nailed it down with his 'they offered me a fix, no it was all a joke' story. The coach who can get goals out of David again will get to speak first at the

NASL awards banquet. Smith yells insults at his non-striking teammates and throws shirts at Hubert Vogelsinger. Being flaky does not necessarily mean being dumb."

BEST PLACE TO PLAY

1. Giants' Stadium, New Jersey
2. Tampa Stadium, Tampa Bay
3. Commonwealth Stadium, Edmonton
4. Empire Stadium, Vancouver
5. The Kingdome, Seattle

Notes Pouncey: "For the field, setting, atmosphere, and locker rooms, Giants' Stadium is No. 1. Plus, it's not in New York. Everything is first class in Tampa Bay, and Edmonton's new stadium is gorgeous. Now that soccer has made it to Vancouver, the atmosphere may be the best in the whole league."

WORST PLACE TO PLAY

1. Holleder Stadium, Rochester
2. Ownby Stadium, Dallas
3. Spartan Stadium, San Jose
4. Civic Stadium, Portland
5. Soldier Field, Chicago

Notes Pouncey: "It's not just Holleder Stadium in Rochester; it's the city, the fans, the team. Ownby Stadium has the worst field, especially in the spring before the grass starts growing. San Jose has atmosphere—maybe too much of it, considering how close the Earthquake boosters are to the players. Civic Stadium field is still badly in need of replacement, and the best thing that could happen to Soldier Field is a time bomb."

MOST POORLY RUN FRANCHISES

1. Philadelphia
2. Houston
3. Memphis
4. Rochester
5. Tulsa

CUTEST TEAM

1. Tampa Bay Rowdies
2. Minnesota Kicks
3. The Cosmos
4. Vancouver Whitecaps
5. New England Tea Men

Notes Pouncey: "This list is for the ladies, compiled by some of the most ardent female fans, counting uniform and off-field garb and just sex appeal.

"Some lists," Pouncey adds, "were simply incomplete or did not require amplification, such as: best broadcaster—Paul Gardner; most intellectual player—Tony Chursky; best interview—Kyle Rote, Jr. (teammate Kai Haaskivi, runnerup); best coach—Tony Waiters and Rinus Michels (tie); best-looking women at the post-game party—Tampa Bay."

SOURCE: *The Complete Handbook of Soccer.*

Real Names of 13 Well-Known Soccer Players

1. Pelé (Edson Arantes do Nascimento)
2. Eusebio (Eusebio Ferreira)
3. Mirandinha (Sabastiao Miranda do Silva Filho)
4. Parviz (Parviz Ghylichkhani)
5. Humberto (Humberto Coelho)
6. Nana (Joseph Gyau)
7. Oreco (Waldemar Rodrigues Martins)
8. Seninho (Arsenio Jardim)
9. Uriel (Uriel da Veiga Fontoura)
10. Vava (Edvaldo Neto)
11. Julie Veee (Gyula Visnyei)
12. Zemaria (Zemaria dos Santos)
13. Rildo (Rildo Memezes)

Jerry Trecker's 7 Greatest Soccer Memories

For 25 years, Jerry Trecker has led a double life as a Connecticut high school teacher and soccer writer. He covers international soccer for the *Hartford* (Conn.) *Courant* and contributes regularly to *Soccer Digest* and *Soccer Monthly.* He also has covered the sport for the British Broadcasting Company's World Service.

1. June 7, 1970—Sitting with 20,000 fans in Madison Square Garden to watch via television, as Brazil beat England in the 1970 World Cup. That was the afternoon it became apparent I wasn't crazy; or at least there were others who knew there

The incomparable Pelé.
Rich Pilling

10
19

was a World Cup taking place. Nobody at school had been able to understand that I was going to New York to see a television show from Mexico. They probably still don't.

2. August 27, 1976—Seeing Bayern Munich in the Olympiastadion, just months before the great European championship side was to begin breaking up. It was a rare treat to see Franz Beckenbauer, Gerd Muller, Uli Hoeness, and Sepp Maier, not knowing that only one would be left with the team within a span of 36 months. That night, they drew with Eintracht Braunschweig, 2-2.
3. August 13, 1977—The F.A. Charity Shield at Wembley Stadium, London. There is no atmosphere like Wembley, no arena that seems to trap the sound and turn it against itself. Two and a half hours of sound and color, no goals between Liverpool and Manchester United, but noboby asked for a shoot-out, either.
4. August 4, 1979—Rangers 3, Celtics 1, at Hampden Park, Glasgow. It almost defied description. If you haven't seen this game, you cannot possibly fathom what's going on in Scottish soccer.
5. October 1, 1977—Pelé's last game, his final goal, Giants Stadium, East Rutherford, N.J. Stage-managed perfectly, the day still managed to rise above its planning, and the reason was simple: Pelé was genuine, and even the hard-bitten news hounds craned their necks for a final look in that emotional press-room session after the game.
6. August 12, 1973—The second greatest day in United States' soccer history: US 1, Poland 0, in New Britain, Conn. Even today, people don't know that that really was the Polish national team that was Olympic champion in 1972, World Cup third-placers in 1974. It was. We won. Believe it.
7. Any afternoon when the players function as a team, lifting their effort to produce something just a bit special. So fluid and graceful is the sport that it can happen on any level.

Barry Janoff's 13 Soccer Players Who Know Their Game

Barry Janoff is a West Coast freelance writer who specializes in soccer and has a fascination for names.

1. Alan Ball
2. Tony Field
3. Jose Neto
4. Peter Wall

5. Lee Atack
6. Stewart Jump
7. Chris Dangerfield
8. David Robb
9. David Stride
10. Paul Crossley
11. Phil Holder
12. Curtis Leeper
13. Dave Power

EDITORS' NOTE: Special mention to Trevor Hockey.

Secretariat defeats Sham in the 1973 Kentucky Derby.

Louisville Courier-Journal

XII

Back In The Saddle

Sam "The Genius" Lewin's 10 Greatest Thoroughbreds, Trainers, and Jockeys of All Time

For more than half a century, Sam "The Genius" Lewin has been affiliated with racing as a stable manager, handicapper, and author. He discovered Bill Hartack on a small track in Charlestown, W. Va., and brought him to major league racing. He later discovered Howard Grant on the same track. Lewin is the author of the book *The Education of a Horse Player*.

THOROUGHBREDS

1. Count Fleet
2. Native Dancer
3. Forego
4. Affirmed
5. Seattle Slew
6. Seabiscuit
7. Man O' War
8. Secretariat
9. Reigh Count
10. Ruffian

Lewin notes: "Count Fleet is the greatest horse of all time. Without Native Dancer, we never would have had Affirmed. I hesitate about Secretariat. A great horse, but I'm not sure the top 10 should include a horse who never raced beyond a three-year old. Ruffian is the only filly on the list. I have omitted Citation, which might surprise some people. But he was greatly overrated. He never beat a decent horse, and any time he faced one, he was beat."

TRAINERS

1. Hirsch Jacobs
2. Allen Jerkens
3. Laz Barrera
4. Cecil Whittingham
5. Devern Emery
6. J. Boes Bond
7. Horatio Luro
8. Sam Hildreth
9. Fred Hopkins
10. Preston Burch

Says Lewin: "Hirsch Jacobs was the best of all time, although he never won a Derby or a Preakness. He should have won the Derby with Personality. Hirsch was the victim of a lot of jealousy. He had the reputation of winning only with claimers, that he never produced a great horse. They said he never produced a two-year old, and he came up with Affectionately. Then they said he never had a three-year old, and he trained Hail to Reason. He was 11 times leading trainer in the country."

JOCKEYS

1. Willie Shoemaker
2. Bill Hartack
3. Johnny Longden
4. Eddie Arcaro
5. Earl Sande
6. Levern Fator
7. Jackie Westrope
8. Lafitt Pincay
9. Jorge Velasquez
10. Angel Cordero

Says Lewin: "Who can argue with Shoe as No. 1? Hartack was the greatest handicapper among jockeys. He never took a mount if he didn't think the horse could win. He won five Kentucky Derbies and refused Derby mounts because he didn't think the horse had a chance. Arcaro is the most overrated rider. When he rode, there were no other good riders around."

Jim Bolus' 15 Favorite Names of Kentucky Derby Starters, and How They Got Them

Jim Bolus, of the *Louisville Times,* a former publicity director at Churchill Downs, is author of *Run for the Roses,* a history of the Kentucky Derby. Bolus and colleague Billy Reed won a National

Headliners Club Award for outstanding investigative reporting and a Sigma Delta Chi Distinguished Service Award for general reporting. Both awards stemmed from 1972 investigative stories on the Kentucky Derby thoroughbred industry. Bolus is the only three-time winner of the annual turf-writing contest, sponsored by the Florida Thoroughbred Breeders' Assn. and the Ocala-Marion County Chamber of Commerce.

1. Seattle Slew (1977)—The name reflected the home area of his owners, Mickey and Karen Taylor, from the state of Washington, and Jim Hill, from southern Florida, where swamp sloughs (or slews) abound. The owners wanted a snappy name and, explains Karen Taylor, "White Swan Slew —that's the little town we're from in Washington—didn't sound right, so we called him . . . well, you know."
2. Amano (1976)—Owner Jim Irvin explained that chauvinism led to this acronym.

   "My secretary, Rita Cutbush, and I argued about this women's lib stuff," Irvin explained.

   So, when he sent names to The Jockey Club for approval, Irvin tried several variations of "Male Chauvinist." Each was rejected.

   "Then one day I came to the office and there was Rita asleep, with her head on the typewriter. I said, 'Hell, women aren't equal to men.' So I wrote out, 'All Men Are Number One.' Then I took the first letter from each word. I gave it to Rita to send in. After a long time, I still hadn't heard anything from The Jockey Club. Rita had the name in her desk. She had refused to send it in."
3. Foolish Pleasure (1975)—How did this son of What a Pleasure get his name?

   "Well," owner John Greer said in 1975, "I married my present wife two years ago. She's my third wife, and she's younger than I am, so I teased her by saying it was quite appropriate that I, marrying a young wife, should name that horse Foolish Pleasure. Actually, he gets his name from What a Pleasure and his dam, Fool-Me-Not. So Foolish Pleasure was a natural for him."
4. Prince Thou Art (1975)—From the poem, "The Barefoot Boy," by John Greenleaf Whittier. Prince Thou Art's disappointing out-of-the-money finishes in all three triple-crown

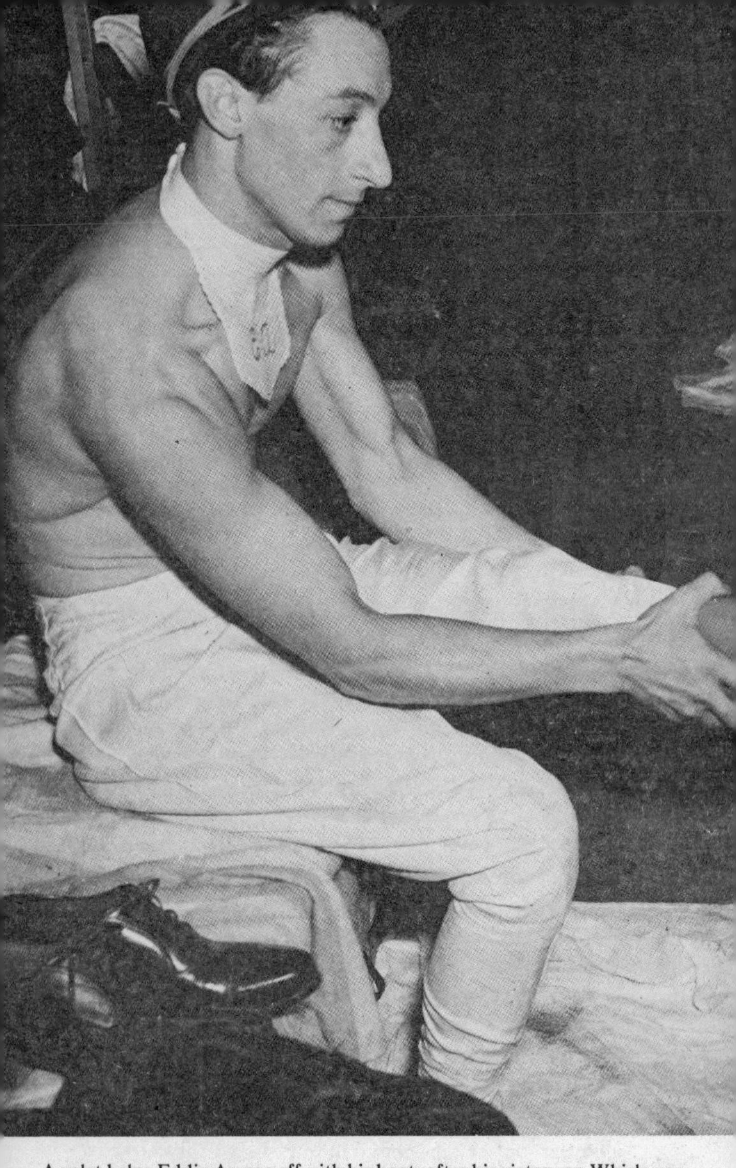

A valet helps Eddie Arcaro off with his boot, after his victory on Whirlaway in 1941, one of five Kentucky Derby winners for Arcaro.

Louisville Courier-Journal

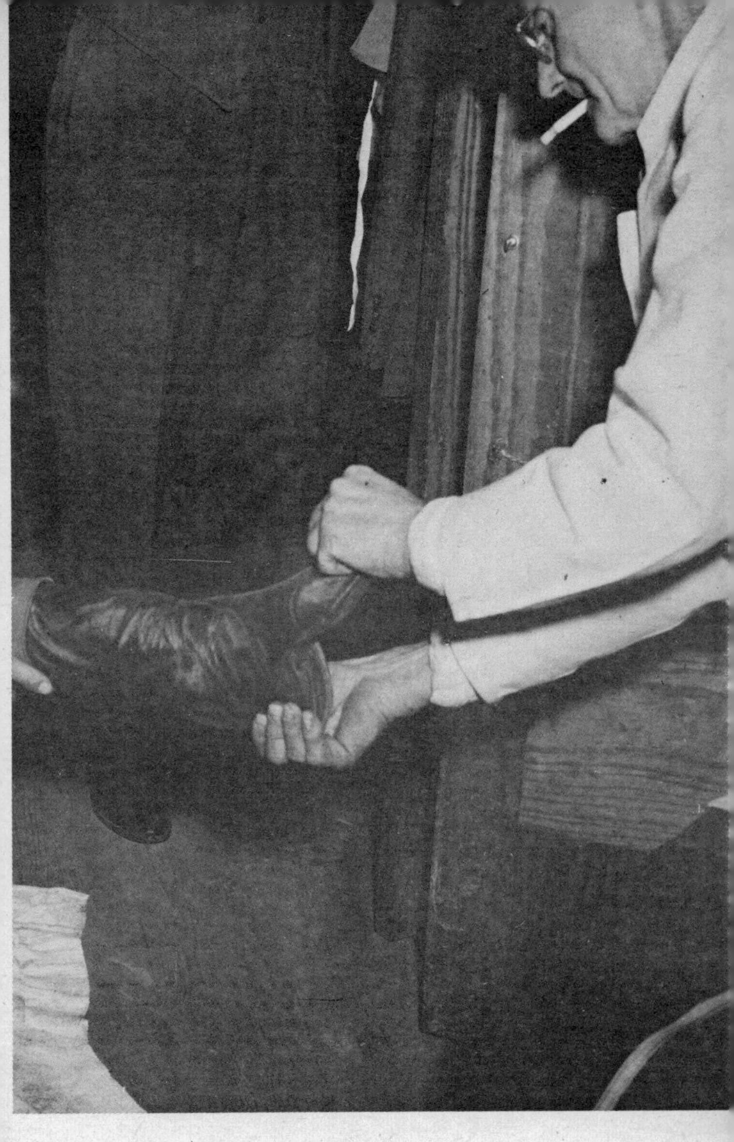

races led some who had wagered on him to suggest a new name—Prince Thou Ain't.

5. Consigliori (1974)—In an alibi column after the Derby, Mike Barry, of the *Louisville Times,* wrote of this 20th-place finisher: "Named for a character in *The Godfather.* His jockey's plan was to shoot all the other riders, but he could never get within range."
6. Shecky Greene (1973)—Named by owner Joe Kellman after the comedian, who said: "Lucky they didn't use my real name. Can you imagine rooting for a horse called Sheldon Greenfield?"
7. Trouble Brewing (1968)—His pedigree—by Gallant Man out of Sizzling—"seemed to fit very well with Trouble Brewing," noted William Stirling, the colt's trainer. Stirling added that the first choice—Man in a Hurry—"was turned down by The Jockey Club for other obvious reasons."
8. The Scoundrel (1964)—The name, suggested by a friend of owner Rex Ellsworth, was an interesting one and was given to a young horse with some potential. The *Miami News'* Tommy Fitzgerald added a new twist to the name immediately after the Derby.

   "No matter what the record book will show or what you happen to hear," Fitzgerald wrote, "sports writers will remember the 90th Kentucky Derby as the year the Scoundrel won and also finished third."

   The Scoundrel—the four-legged one, that is—finished third. The other one, otherwise known as Bill Hartack, rode Northern Dancer to victory. Following the Derby, it seems Hartack was in no hurry to meet the press. Instead, he stayed outside the jockeys' room signing autographs. Almost an hour after the race, Hartack finally entered the room. No wonder deadline-minded turf writers called Hartack "The Scoundrel," among other things.
9. Carry Back (1961)—So named "because we had a few years of losses in the horse business and we hoped this colt would win enough so that we could carry back those profits to the loss years," according to trainer Jack Price, whose wife, Katherine, raced Carry Back in her name. With Carry Back earning $1,241,165 in purses, the Prices accomplished their purpose..

Price added that Matt Reddy, the groom for Carry Back, had another version of how the horse was named. "He claimed that Mrs. Price named him that because I had to be carried back home after a few drinks."

10. Bally Ache (1960)—"We sent in four beautiful names—Bali Hai, Bally Lad, Bally Dancer, and another one," said Leonard Fruchtman, who owned Bally Ache, a son of Ballydam. Fruchtman and his trainer, Jimmy Pitt, were trying to think of another name before submitting their list to The Jockey Club.

    "You know," Pitt said, "just thinkin' of names, a guy can get a belly ache."

    "That's your fifth name," Fruchtman said. "They won't take it, anyway."

    With a chuckle, Fruchtman later recalled, "Darn if The Jockey Club didn't come up with the worst name on the list."

11. Silky Sullivan (1958)—Sire: Sullivan; dam: Lady N Silk. Comedian George Jessel cracked that the colt's real name was Silky Solomon, but that he had been horsenapped by the Irish.

12. Needles (1956)—A widely circulated story held that Needles derived his name from the many injections he received when he was an unhealthy foal. However, other sources insist that Needles got his name because, as a frisky youngster, he needled and pestered other horses in the paddock.

    Years after the '56 Derby, Howard Cosell applied his own wrinkle to Needles' name. On a national telecast, Cosell referred to this famous champion, this Kentucky Derby and Belmont winner, as "Noodles."

    I wonder if Cosell likes "needle soup" for lunch?

13. Lee O. Cotner (1925)—Kentucky State steward Keene Daingerfield explains that this Derby starter was a namesake of an Indiana man who owned the horse's dam, Precious Pearl. "She was double-bred, and Lee O. Cotner is registered by Last Coin or High Time," Daingerfield noted. "Mr. Cotner, the owner, was unfortunately sent to the Indiana State Penitentiary for some offense I do not recall, and it was one of the conditions of the sale of the horse that it be named after him. He said at the time, 'If I'm going to be just a number for five years, I want my name on the outside.' "

14. Revenue Agent (1924)—This horse couldn't have had a more fitting name. His owner, Gifford A. Cochran, was jailed by revenue agents for possession of whiskey at Churchill Downs on Derby Day, 1924. A year later, Cochran's victory with Flying Ebony prompted a cartoonist to draw a clever caricature of the owner with the caption: "Last year, the jug; this year, the mug."
15. Ben Brush (1896)—Named after Ben Brush, the Gravesend racetrack superintendent who disliked having dogs at his track, but who made an exception in the case of horseman Eugene Leigh. As a young colt, Ben Brush was owned by Leigh and Ed Brown, the latter being responsible for naming the horse in honor of Brush.

    "Mr. Brush is a mighty nice man," Brown said. "He gave me stalls once when stable room was mighty scarce, and was mighty clever to me."

    Brush frequently complained to other horsemen about their dogs roaming the track grounds. Finally, they asked him, "Why are Eugene Leigh's dogs allowed to run all over the track and even walk on the lawn?"

    "Not a damn one of you fellows ever named a horse Ben Brush," the superintendent retorted.

Patrick Premo's 18 Thoroughbreds Who Never Lost a Race

Patrick Premo, of Allegheny, N.Y., is a horse-racing buff.

Horse	Races	Year Foaled	Country
1. Kincsem	54	1874	Hungary
2. Eclipse	18	1764	England
3. Ormonde	16	1883	England
4. Ribot	16	1952	Italy
5. Colin	15	1905	United States
6. Nearco	14	1935	Italy
7. Tremont	13	1884	United States
8. Asteroid	12	1861	United States
9. Barcaldine	12	1878	Ireland
10. Kurifuji	10	1940	Japan
11. St. Simon	10	1881	England
12. Tokino Minoru	10	1948	Japan
13. Bahram	9	1932	England
14. American Eclipse	8	1814	United States
15. The Tetrarch	7	1911	England
16. Hurry On	6	1913	England
17. Norfolk	4	1861	United States
18. Flying Childers	?	1715	England

Premo adds: "There is no record on how many races Flying Childers won. The other 17 horses won a total of 234 races in 234 starts."

Bjorn Borg at Wimbledon. *UPI*

XIII

Match Point!

Lance Tingay's 10 Greatest Matches at Wimbledon

Lance Tingay, of the *London Daily Telegraph,* has been covering tennis since 1932 and has been on the scene at every Wimbledon tournament since 1955. He is the author of two books on tennis, *100 Years of Wimbledon* and *The Pictorial History of Lawn Tennis.*

(Listed Chronologically)

1. 1883—First round men's singles. Ernest Renshaw beat Herbert Lawford, 5-6, 6-1, 3-6, 6-1, 6-5.
2. 1919—Challenge round women's singles. Suzanne Lenglen beat Dorothea Lambert Chambers, 10-8, 4-6, 9-7.
3. 1927—Semi-final men's singles. Henri Cochet beat Bill Tilden, 2-6, 4-6, 7-5, 6-4, 6-3.
4. 1933—Final men's singles. Jack Crawford beat Ellsworth Vines, 4-6, 11-9, 6-2, 2-6, 6-4.
5. 1935—Final women's singles. Helen Wills Moody beat Helen Jacobs, 6-3, 3-6, 7-5.
6. 1953—Third round men's singles. Jaroslav Drobny beat Budge Patty, 8-6, 16-18, 3-6, 8-6, 12-10.
7. 1969—First round men's singles. Pancho Gonzales beat Charlie Pasarell, 22-24, 1-6, 16-14, 6-3, 11-9.
8. 1970—Final women's singles. Margaret Court beat Billie Jean King, 14-12, 11-9.

9. 1972—Final men's singles. Stan Smith beat Ilie Nastase, 4-6, 6-3, 6-3, 4-6, 7-5.
10. 1979—Semi-final men's singles. Bjorn Borg beat Vitas Gerulaitis, 6-4, 3-6, 6-3, 3-6, 8-6.

Steve Flink's Top 10 Men and Top 10 Women Tennis Players of the 1970s

Steve Flink is an associate editor at *World Tennis* magazine. He has worked as a statistician for NBC, ABC, CBS, and the BBC during tennis telecasts and has rarely missed a Wimbledon or a U.S. Open since 1965.

MEN

1. Bjorn Borg
2. Jimmy Connors
3. Ken Rosewall
4. Ilie Nastase
5. John Newcombe
6. Stan Smith
7. Guillermo Vilas
8. Arthur Ashe
9. Manuel Orantes
10. Jan Kodes

Notes Flink: "Although Borg won the last four Wimbledons, four French Opens, two Italian, and a WCT final, his record was only slightly better than Connors', in my opinion. If Connors had been able to win one more Wimbledon (he won in 1974), it might have been enough to lift him past Borg. Or if he had been able to maintain his early dominance of Borg, it might have put him over the top. After leading, 7-1, in the Rivalry of the Seventies, Connors lost nine of the next 12 encounters to Borg.

"Veterans Rosewall, Nastase, Newcombe, and Smith enjoyed most of their success in the early part of the decade."

WOMEN

1. Chris Evert Lloyd
2. Margaret Court
3. Billie Jean King
4. Evonne Goolagong Cawley
5. Martina Navratilova
6. Virginia Wade
7. Kerry Reid
8. Rosie Casals
9. Tracy Austin
10. Wendy Turnbull

Notes Flink: "Chris Evert Lloyd was unquestionably the best woman player of the seventies. Across the decade, she won more

Chris Evert Lloyd: best in the 1970s.
UPI

than 90 tournaments and compiled a record of 663-61. The Floridian stood in a class of her own.

"Court had a slight edge over King. Austin, picked ninth for the decade, was only 16 and nearing her peak as the decade ended."

Steve Flink's 10 Best Tennis Matches of the 1970s

1. Ken Rosewall defeated Rod Laver, 4-6, 6-0, 6-3, 6-7, 7-6, in the WCT Finals in Dallas, 1972.
2. Chris Evert defeated Martina Navratilova, 7-5, 5-7, 13-11, in the final at Eastbourne, England, 1979.
3. Margaret Court defeated Billie Jean King, 14-12, 11-9, in the final at Wimbledon, 1970.
4. Stan Smith defeated Ilie Nastase, 4-6, 6-3, 6-3, 4-6, 7-5, in the final at Wimbledon, 1972.
5. Margaret Court defeated Chris Evert, 7-6, 6-7, 6-4, in the final of the French Open in Paris, 1973.
6. Jimmy Connors defeated Bjorn Borg, 6-4, 3-6, 7-6, 6-4, in the final of the U.S. Open, Forest Hills, 1976.
7. Billie Jean King defeated Evonne Goolagong, 3-6, 6-3, 7-5, in the final of the U.S. Open, Forest Hills, 1974.
8. Bjorn Borg defeated Vitas Gerulaitis, 6-4, 3-6, 6-3, 3-6, 8-6, in the semifinals at Wimbledon, 1977.
9. Chris Evert defeated Evonne Goolagong, 6-3, 4-6, 8-6, in the final at Wimbledon, 1976.
10. Arthur Ashe defeated Jimmy Connors, 6-1, 6-1, 5-7, 6-4, in the final at Wimbledon, 1975.

XIV

The Fourth Estate

Bill Gallo's 11 Easiest Sports Faces to Draw

Cartoonist extraordinaire Bill Gallo, of the *New York Daily News*, has an eye for faces. "There are people in sports who are easy to capture because of certain characteristics—such as Casey Stengel's ears, Wilt Chamberlain's bandana, Don King's hair, Howard Coseli's nose, and Muhammad Ali's mouth," says Gallo. Herewith, his 11 easiest faces.

1. Casey Stengel
2. Yogi Berra
3. Joe Namath
4. Howard Cosell
5. Muhammad Ali
6. Billy Martin
7. Reggie Jackson
8. Don King
9. George Steinbrenner
10. M. Donald Grant
11. Wilt Chamberlain

The 10 Most Powerful Baseball Writers In America

(Listed Alphabetically)

1. Hal Bock, Baseball Editor, Associated Press: Bock's two columns every week, called "Bock's Score," might well be the most influential baseball pieces written at any given time, simply because of the sheer number of people he reaches.

Casey Stengel

Wilt Chamberlain

Yogi Berra

Reggie Jackson

Howard Cosell

Joe Namath

George Steinbrenner

Muhammad Ali

Don King

Billy Martin

M. Donald Grant

BILL GALLO

The AP wire is carried by some 1,700 newspapers all over the world, more than any other single news service. By AP count, Hal Bock has a potential of 100 million readers.

2. Bob Broeg, Sports Editor, *St. Louis Post-Dispatch:* In addition to the column he writes for his paper, Broeg wrote a column for 10 years for *The Sporting News.* He sits on the important Veterans Committee for the Hall of Fame.
3. Murray Chass, *New York Times:* Writing for as prestigious a newspaper as the *New York Times,* with a daily circulation of one million and 1.5 million on Sunday, Chass has taken the time to become one of the country's most respected writers on the labor issues involved in the game.
4. Joe Falls, *Detroit News:* For the past 23 years, Falls has worked for three Detroit papers, and is currently with the *News,* the paper with the largest evening circulation in America. His column has also appeared in *The Sporting News* for the past 15 years.
5. Peter Gammons, *Boston Globe;* Rarely has a baseball writer established as high a reputation as quickly as 34-year-old Gammons. Part of the reason for Gammons' success is both the singular Boston audience, which tends to take baseball as seriously as it does matters of national security, and the other members of the *Globe* staff, rated the top sports staff in the nation by a 1978 *Time* magazine poll.
6. Jerome Holtzman, *Chicago Sun-Times:* He is more than a baseball writer, he is a baseball scholar, and general opinion has it that he's the finest in the game today. He has what might be the finest private collection of baseball material in the country, including, for example, nine bound volumes of the transcript of the Kuhn-Finley trial. The collection is so large, he cannot estimate how many books are in it. Holtzman is perhaps best known, however, for his 25,000-word "Review of the Year," for the *Baseball Guide.* It takes two months to write, and it chronicles all the developments in and around the game for the year.
7. Jack Lang, *New York Daily News:* Certainly a fellow who has regularly been on the baseball beat for 30 years, works for a paper with a daily circulation of nearly two million (three million on Sunday), and files weekly reports in *The Sporting News* might be considered influential. But in Lang's case, all those outlets pale beside his real power. He is the national

secretary-treasurer of the Baseball Writers Association of America, the most influential group of its kind.

8. Phil Pepe, *New York Daily News:* Author of 15 books, most of them on baseball, and regular beat writer covering the Yankees, the most-written-about team in sports history, Pepe is also the Yankee correspondent for *The Sporting News.*
9. Milt Richman, Sports Editor, United Press International: Born in the shadow of Yankee Stadium, he has made an enviable reputation as a first-rate breaker of stories. He had Durocher leaving the Giants in 1955, Finley moving to Oakland, Bob Feller on waivers, Aaron to Milwaukee—all before everybody else. His friends and sources in baseball are limitless.
10. Dick Young, Sports Editor, *New York Daily News:* Young was inducted into the Hall of Fame in August, 1979, one of a handful of writers to receive the J. G. Taylor Spink Memorial Award for baseball journalists. His column, "Young Ideas," was named the most popular in *The Sporting News* in a reader survey.

SOURCE: *Baseball* magazine.

34 Writers and Photographers Who Have Covered Every Super Bowl

1. Edgar Allen, *Nashville Banner*
2. John Biever, photographer, Port Washington, Wis.
3. Vern Biever, photographer, Port Washington, Wis.
4. Dave Brady, *Washington Post*
5. Si Burick, *Dayton Daily News*
6. Bob Burnes, *St. Louis Globe-Democrat*
7. Dick Connor, *Denver Post*
8. Art Daley, *Green Bay Press Gazette*
9. Malcolm Emmons, photographer, Delaware, Ohio
10. Larry Felser, *Buffalo Evening News*
11. Mel Durslag, *Los Angeles Herald-Examiner*
12. Jerry Green, *Detroit News*
13. Walter Iooss, photographer, *Sports Illustrated*
14. Jerry Izenberg, *Newark Star-Ledger*
15. Ray Kelly, *Camden Courier-Post*
16. Dave Klein, *Newark Star-Ledger*

17. Bud Lea, *Milwaukee Sentinel*
18. Augie Lio, *Passaic Herald*
19. Will McDonough, *Boston Globe*
20. Jim Murray, *Los Angeles Times*
21. Norman Miller, *New York Daily News*
22. Keith Morris, *Sports Illustrated*
23. Jack Murphy, *San Diego Union*
24. Bob Oates, *Los Angeles Times*
25. Mickey Palmer, photographer, New York
26. Dick Peebles, *Houston Chronicle*
27. Ed Pope, *Miami Herald*
28. Dick Raphael, photographer, Marblehead, Mass.
29. Cooper Rollow, *Chicago Tribune*
30. Gene Roswell, *New York Post*
31. John Seguin, Canadian Broadcasting Corp.
32. John Steadman, *Baltimore News-American*
33. Tony Tomsic, photographer, *Cleveland Press*
34. Bill Wallace, *New York Times*

Bill Libby's 15 Good Guys and 15 Bad Guys in Sports

When freelancer Bill Libby first did this list as part of a feature for the *Los Angeles Herald-Examiner,* he stressed the fact that it was about the "good guys" and the "bad guys" in sports, yet he found many misunderstood it to be about the "good interviews" and the "bad interviews."

He says, "Many a good guy is a bad interview, and many a bad guy is a good interview. The good and bad interviews are another story, but this story is about the good and bad guys of fun and games, insofar as the way they treat, or treated, the press and public over the last 30 years. I limited it to stars because the others don't have to deal with the sort of pressure that brings out the best, and the worst, in players."

THE GOOD GUYS

1. Gordie Howe—"Howe will talk to anyone until the rest of the team is on the bus and he has yet to shower and has no way back to the hotel."

2. Reggie Jackson—"Maybe it's his ego, but Reggie Jackson knows a good story and he will give it to the writers whenever they want it. He'll even talk about bad stories being written about him. A lot will talk in the best of times, but it takes class to talk in the worst of times. Reggie has had his run-ins with fans, but only when pressed beyond endurance."
3. O. J. Simpson—"O. J. has never had a run-in with anybody."
4. Richard Petty and Mario Andretti—"Andretti is always available, as are Petty and other racers. Petty is the finest with the fans I've ever seen. No one even comes close. He is super-patient with the people. As a result, he may be the most popular athlete of all time."
5. Steve Garvey—"Steve gets a lot of guff for being 'too good to be true,' but he is interested in the press and public and completely cooperative."
6. Tony Lema
7. Bobby Hull—"I have seen Hull talk to anyone who wanted to talk, when his jaw was broken and wired shut and it was tough to talk."
8. Wilt Chamberlain—"I have had a couple of confrontations with athletes over something I have written. The only one of consequence was with Wilt Chamberlain. When Bill Sharman came to coach Wilt on the Lakers, many of us wrote stories about problems this demanding coach and his temperamental star seemed certain to have. As these stories appeared, Bill and Wilt agreed to prove them wrong. By the time mine appeared, in a magazine which had taken months to print it, they had proven me wrong. At that point, yet another abusive article angered Wilt. 'The same old bleep,' he muttered one night, demanding I depart the dressing room. Well, he was right, I was wrong. I left, but returned the next night. After that, he answered my questions after games without acknowledging me. But he answered. Many would not, but I have to put Wilt on the good side because he always answered all of our questions."
9. John Brodie— "He has had a critical press, but he always conducted himself with class."
10. Rick Barry and Jerry West—"Barry, like Brodie, conducted himself with class despite a critical press. West admits that as a coach he found the press difficult to deal with, but as a

player he made himself available after the most disappointing defeats."

11. Nolan Ryan and Vida Blue—"They are always right there."
12. Rogie Vachon and Marcel Dionne—"Nobody was down farther than Vachon in the 1979 season, but the little guy faced the world like the real man he is."
13. Ernie Banks—"Like Garvey, they say he is 'too good to be true.' But he did not know I was there one morning when he came downstairs beaming joy at 'another beautiful day,' just as he always did in the dugout."
14. Ken Norton—"Ken Norton may have been knocked down and out, but he gets up and is a stand-up guy with the press and public."
15. George McGinnis

THE BAD GUYS

1. Mike Marshall—"They say Mike Marshall is a changed man, but I'll have to see it to believe it; he still tops my list of bad guys. He has been for a long time the athlete most abusive in his dealings with the press. He has considered them with contempt. Considering himself an intellectual aristocrat, he has treated the press as uneducated peasants. But he never succeeded in cutting them down to his size."
2. Terry Sawchuk—"When I first met my boyhood idol and asked as politely as possible for a brief interview, I was told as impolitely as possible to do something anatomically impossible."
3. Danny Ongais—"Car racers are really good as a rule, but Danny Ongais is as bad as a guy can be to reporters. Some yesterdays back, when he was on the way up, he gave me a good interview. But today, when he is at the top, he glares angrily at anyone who approaches him, and grunts his contempt for others."
4. Willie Mays, Mickey Mantle, Roger Maris—"They were good to those major writers who treated them as gods, but terrible to others—thin-skinned, often obscene, too big to be bothered by the little guy. As superstars, they were worshipped by fans, but those few who got close to them found them too hot to touch."
5. Johnny Unitas, Joe Namath, Ken Stabler—"From yesterday to today, the disease of disgust has stricken some superstar

quarterbacks, such as Unitas, Namath, and Stabler. Also Sonny Jurgensen."

6. Duane Thomas—"He wouldn't talk to anybody, not even his coaches, and his silence came with contempt."
7. Oscar Robertson—"Few have been as abusive to others as Oscar Robertson in his heyday."
8. Bob Gibson—"Bob Gibson cursed reporters who tried to talk to him, then turned around and tried to be a reporter who talked to athletes. As a general rule, baseball has had the most abusive athletes."
9. Jim Rice, Dave Kingman, Steve Carlton—"They all but spit at the press and public these days."
10. Kareem Abdul-Jabbar and Bill Walton—"They are teamed because they both studied at the John Wooden School of Silence, but I list them lower than others would because both gave me good, extensive interviews and both are fascinating when you ask them about things other than their sport."
11. Jimmy Connors, Ilie Nastase, John McEnroe—"They are as nasty off the court as they are on it at times."
12. Sugar Ray Robinson—"Boxers are among the best, but Sugar Ray Robinson seldom is sweet."
13. Steve Ovett—"Track stars thirst for recognition, but Steve Ovett is all arrogance and abuse where press and public are concerned, and would rank higher if more recognized."
14. Dave Cowens—"He acts with arrogance the moment he is approached."
15. Ben Hogan—"As a rule, golfers are good, but Ben Hogan was a bad guy."

Muhammad Ali is on the way to his TKO of Joe Frazier in Manila.

UPI

XV

The Manly Art

Sylvester Stallone's 5 Favorite Fights

The author and star of *Rocky* and *Rocky II* is a lifetime boxing fan. He prepared this list for the magazine *Inside Sports*.

1. Marcel Cerdan vs. Tony Zale, September 21, 1948. Cerdan knocked out Zale in the 12th round in Jersey City, N.J., to win the middleweight crown.
2. Muhammad Ali vs. Joe Frazier, October 1, 1975, their third fight, in Manila. Ali won on a technical knockout in the 14th round, to retain his heavyweight championship.
3. Archie Moore vs. Yvon Durelle, December 10, 1958, in Montreal. Moore knocked out Durelle in the 11th round, to retain his light-heavyweight crown.
4. Rocky Marciano vs. Ezzard Charles, their first meeting on June 17, 1954, in New York. Marciano won on a 15-round decision, to retain his heavyweight crown.
5. Lou Ambers vs. Henry Armstrong, August 22, 1939, New York. In a 15-round decision, Ambers won the lightweight championship.

10 Fights Harry Markson Would Have Liked to Promote

Harry Markson spent a lifetime in boxing, starting as a boxing writer in the 1930s. He was hired by Mike Jacobs as publicity director when Jacobs became boxing promoter for Madison Square

Garden in 1937. In 1948, he was named head of Garden boxing and served as president and promoter for the famed "Mecca of Boxing" until his retirement in 1973. He was involved in more championship matches than any other promoter in boxing history. Markson now serves as a consultant to Madison Square Garden boxing.

1. Joe Louis vs. Muhammad Ali
2. Joe Louis vs. Jack Dempsey
3. Muhammad Ali vs. Gene Tunney
4. Rocky Marciano vs. Joe Frazier
5. Ray Robinson vs. Harry Greb
6. Ray Robinson vs. Carlos Monzon
7. Willie Pep vs. Johnny Dundee
8. Roberto Duran vs. Tony Canzoneri
9. Billy Conn vs. Archie Moore
10. Henry Armstrong vs. Sugar Ray Leonard

Markson adds: "None of the 'figment fights' needs explanation, but of Dempsey-Louis, there is this note: I once put the question to each. Said the Brown Bomber: 'I was lucky Dempsey hung up his gloves before I got started.' Said the Manassa Mauler: 'It would have been a toss-up, but one helluva fight while it lasted.' "

Angelo Dundee's 10 Greatest Left-handed Fighters

Closely associated with seven world champions—Muhammad Ali, Jimmy Ellis, Willie Pastrano, Ralph Dupas, Sugar Ramos, Luis Rodriguez, and Carmen Basilio—Angelo Dundee is currently guiding the career of Sugar Ray Leonard. "It's taken years for southpaws to get rid of the stigma of being awkward," he says. "I managed a few southpaws. In boxing, that's a no-no. A successful left-hander should get a medal. It's difficult getting fights and becoming an attraction, because the public doesn't seem to like left-handers. When a guy walks into a gym and he's a southpaw, it casts a pall over the gym. That's why a lot of natural southpaws are immediately converted to right-handed, such as Joe Miceli."

1. Kenny Lane—He was a smooth-working southpaw.
2. Vicente Saldivar
3. Bert Lytell—He was a light heavy who fought heavyweights because he couldn't get people to fight him. Only Archie Moore would fight him in his division.

4. Jimmy Carruthers
5. Melio Bettina
6. Marvin Hagler
7. Irish Bob Murphy—He was exciting because he was a good banger, and the crowd loved him.
8. Chuck Davey—Make no mistake, he could fight, and he packed 'em in because he was a crowd pleaser.
9. Tony Chiaverini—Another current southpaw who has a good following and does good business at the box office.
10. Doc Williams

EDITORS' NOTE: Dundee restricted his list only to fighters of his era. From boxing buff Paul McKenna comes this list of champions who were left-handed.

1. Tiger Flowers
2. Al McCoy
3. Lou Brouillard
4. Jimmy Carruthers
5. Freddie Miller
6. Johnny Wilson
7. Melio Bettina
8. Young Corbett III
9. Billy Backus
10. Vicente Saldivar

Clyde Frazier in his heyday as a New York Knick.

UPI

XVI

Shaping Up

Walt "Clyde" Frazier's 10 Grooming Secrets

With his Rolls Royce, his fur coats, his lavish bachelor pad, and his extensive wardrobe, Clyde Frazier was a *bon vivant,* sex symbol and man-about-Manhattan when he played for the New York Knickerbockers. Good grooming habits helped make it happen.

1. Every morning, when I wake up, I go through a routine. I get out of bed, stand, and bend low from the waist. This gets the blood flowing through my body.
2. Still in that position, I give my head a fingertip massage. Then I pull my hair and knead my scalp. This is good for the circulation of the head and hair. Not long ago, my hair started falling out. I got a book on how to save your hair. It was a necessity. Can you imagine a bald Clyde? The book's suggestions have straightened out the problem. After the massage, I use the 100-stroke system with the brush. All this takes about five minutes, and it all takes place in the bending-over position.
3. I take a lukewarm shower, then a cold shower. Stimulates the blood, and that's good for the complexion.
4. I dry my body with a stiff towel, and use short, brisk movements. That "beats the blood up," too. But I use a soft towel on my face, and I dab, I don't rub, which irritates the skin.
5. I don't use much soap on my face, maybe once a week at the most. Soap dries the skin out.

6. Every morning, I squeeze a towel with water as hot as I can stand it on my face. Then I use a cold towel on my face. I rotate each towel about two or three times a minute. It helps circulation by opening and closing the pores.
7. I don't usually like lotions on my body because it makes my clothes feel sweaty. But I sometimes use Noxema on my face.
8. I slap cologne all over my body; lookin' good, smellin' fine.
9. I keep my fingernails short, for two reasons. One, I don't want to cut up somebody on the court. Another is that I wear a lot of knits, so short nails are an economy move. I'm afraid that with long nails I'd be tearing up my clothes.
10. I do facial exercises. I stretch my mouth—it looks like I'm yawning. I blow up my cheeks, like I'm carrying two cheekloads of water. These two exercises help keep the facial skin tight. I also squinch my eyes very tight, and then I open them wide. That relaxes the eyes. I do the eye and facial exercises whenever I have a spare moment. I avoid doing it in places like a crowded elevator. You can get some pretty queer stares.

SOURCE: *Rockin' Steady,* by Walt Frazier and Ira Berkow (Prentice-Hall).

LeRoy Neiman's 5 Sexiest Women in Sports

Although his work is not restricted to sports, LeRoy Neiman is America's foremost artist on the sports scene. He also is known to have an eye for women, and says he prefers to sketch women live. "Lately, I've started to draw more women," he says. "I've had bad luck with basketball players, but I'm going to keep trying." His selections are restricted only to women he's drawn.

1. Laura Baugh (golfer)—"Blonde and dimpled."
2. Robyn Smith (jockey)—"A good seat."
3. Nancy Lopez (golfer)—"Abundant, and all good form."
4. Diane Morrison (tennis player)—"Smooth and feline."
5. Gigi Fernandez (tennis player)—"A distraction in any mixed doubles match."

Jayne Kennedy's 9 Sexiest Men in Sports

For the past two seasons, beauteous Jayne Kennedy has brightened the TV screen on *CBS NFL Today.* She has also appeared in a television movie, *The Mysterious Island of Beautiful Women,* and on episodes of *CHIPS* and *Trapper John.* Her list, in no order

Laura Baugh: sexy in the trap.

UPI

of preference, is restricted to football players, with one notable exception.

1. O. J. Simpson—"He's all-around charismatically sexy."
2. Franco Harris—"He's got the sexiest eyes I've ever seen."
3. Thomas Henderson—"There's so much character in his face."
4. Tim Foley—"I don't know why, he just is."
5. Walt Garrison—"He's the epitome of gentleman sexy; very distinguished."
6. Jim Zorn—"He's All-American sexy."
7. Danny White—"I like his hair."
8. Gerald Irons—"He's got one of the best bodies in the NFL."
9. Muhammad Ali—"A total person."

Bill Starr's 10 Golden Rules of Rehabilitation for the Injured Athlete

1. Do not diagnose your own injury.
2. Check with your doctor for diagnoses.
3. Do not exercise any injury that results in a lot of pain.
4. If weight training is in order, use high repetitions (low weight) for the first week of rehabilitation.
5. Work directly on the injured area.
6. Exercise the injured area every day during rehabilitation.
7. The injured area should receive exercise priority.
8. Progressively lower the repetitions and increase weight.
9. Pay special attention to good diet and nutrition during the recovery period.
10. Keep in constant touch with the medical expert.

SOURCE: *The Strongest Shall Survive,* by Bill Starr (Fitness Products Limited).

The 8 Greatest Training Rules of the Roaring '90s, as Prescribed by Top Professional Trainer W. W. Morgan, That Stand the Least Chance of Being Adopted in 1980

1. Take a black draught every evening. (Black draught is a very active and nasty-tasting cathartic.)

O. J. Simpson: dressed to kill.
NBC

2. In the morning when you first get up, take a drink of hard cider, or sherry and egg. Then take a sponge bath and rub with a coarse towel.
3. For breakfast, eat a beefsteak cooked rare, and stale bread. Use no milk, sugar, butter, or potatoes, except an ounce per week.
4. For dinner, eat rare roast beef and stale bread. Don't eat any potatoes or vegetables of any kind with this meal.
5. For supper, eat a lean steak or mutton chop without fat. Eat no pies or pastry of any kind.
6. Drink sparingly of water.
7. Do not eat beans or vegetables of any kind except an occasional raw onion.
8. If you feel weak in the morning, it comes from bathing. Do not bathe for a few days.

Professor Morgan's prescription for a rub to harden the muscles: arnica flowers, borax, Jamaica rum, and hartshorn liniment. (Rumor has it that when Professor Morgan was training the well-known All-American W. C. Fields, this prescription was delivered in a tankard.)

SOURCE: *Scholastic Coach* magazine.

Dr. Allan J. Ryan's 4 Medical Sports Myths About the Care and Feeding of Athletes

"I'm not sure how these things get started, but they persist from generation to generation," says Dr. Ryan of Minneapolis, who has been involved in sports medicine for more than two decades. "Some have been handed down from ancient Greece."

1. Overheated athletes shouldn't drink liquids, particularly cold drinks, during breaks in competition.

   "In the old days, athletes were advised not to drink any liquids at all while competing or practicing. They were told they'd become water-logged and suffer stomach cramps. It's all nonsense, because most people lose more in sweat in hot weather than they can replace quickly, even by drinking freely of water or fruit juice or whatever. When you're dehydrated, water is absorbed very rapidly. And later there were injunctions against drinking cold water. At one time, they said if you take any water during exercise, it should be at room temperature. That's silly, because if your temperature is going up, as it always does during exercise, if you drink cold water it helps bring your body temperature down."

2. For energy, athletes should load up on proteins, particularly red meat.

   "The red-meat diet goes back to the ancient Greeks. But an athlete gets all the protein he needs from the meat and other items in his regular diet. Actually, what they need for energy is more carbohydrates. This is where they tend to short themselves, particularly on eating vegetables and fruits and cereals, which should be their main source of carbohydrates."

3. Women can't stand physical stress the way men can.

   "More women are engaged in vigorous sports than ever before, and we have enough experience now to show they are just as capable as men under extreme stress. They do not have enough male hormones to develop great muscle so they never can have the same strength per pound of weight as a conditioned male. But many trained female athletes are stronger than the average man."

4. Women who engage in vigorous athletics will reduce their ability to bear children.

   "We found that not to be true. In fact, they not only are equally able to conceive but often have less difficulty in pregnancy and labor. Not long ago, I saw a picture of a rodeo cowgirl in her eighth month of pregnancy competing in a bucking bronco event. That's carrying it a bit to the extreme, in my opinion, but it shows what women are doing these days."

SOURCE: United Press International.

The seasons at Dartmouth. *Dartmouth*

XVII

Halls Of Ivy

Stan and Natalie Isaacs' 12 Most Beautiful College Campuses in the Land

Sports columnist Stan Isaacs, of *Newsday,* has touched bases at college-stadium press boxes and coops on campuses across the land. He and his wife, Natalie, have made campus scouting trips to select colleges for their progeny, and the family has, in all, graced the campuses of Brooklyn College, Stanford, Champlain College, UCLA, Berkeley, Columbia, Albany State, Union, Brown, and Framingham State.

1. Dartmouth
2. Stanford
3. Haverford
4. West Point
5. Princeton
6. (tie) William and Mary, Virginia
8. California at Berkeley
9. Hamilton
10. Annapolis
11. Colgate
12. Air Force Academy

10 Sure Ways for the Athletic Director to Make His Coaches Hate Him

Jim Neff, of Cadillac High School in Cadillac, Mich., prepared this list and the one that follows for *Scholastic Coach* magazine.

1. If the coach's wife comes to the game, require her to pay to get in: The fact that she's the coach's wife should entitle her to no better treatment than the average fan. After all, the coach has done all the work; she just rides along on his coattails. Besides, the passes have to be saved for important people, like principals and superintendents.
2. Have no policy for fund disbursement: Determine the needs of each sport yourself and order accordingly. Don't ask for input from the coaches; they'll only ask for more than they deserve. And, after all, you know which sports are important and which are not.
3. Let special-interest groups "donate" to their pet sport: Make sure the coaches know that all booster-club monies must be routed through you for use in the overall sports program. But if a particular team winds up with items that you didn't buy, don't investigate or press the issue. When the baseball coach (whose team wears 10-year-old uniforms) asks how the ski team can afford new sweaters every year, tell him you have no idea. You're the A.D, not Barnaby Jones.
4. Tell coaches how to coach: Every coach wants to know what you would have done in last week's game. Volunteer stories about how things would have been handled in "your day"—when the schedule was tougher and the talent was thinner and you always won with superior strategy. If you've never had any coaching experience, offer technical advice based on the expertise you've acquired through listening to Howard Cosell.
5. Use hearsay and opinion as assessment tools in coaching evaluations: Don't observe practices yourself. You've got more important things to do, like counting gate receipts. You can get an accurate-enough picture of the coach's effectiveness by polling parents who go to practice. Besides, you can ultimately tell if the coach isn't practicing right by his won-lost percentage.
6. Differentiate between major and minor sports: Some coaches fail to realize that money is the bottom line. Sports

that don't bring in revenue don't deserve the same status as those that do. The cross-country coach must understand this when his team is denied meal money while the football team is fed before and after the game.

7. Don't consult the head coach when hiring assistants: Any assistant who agrees with your philosophy is good enough for the head coach. Given a choice between two assistants, pick the one who's less likely to "rock the boat"—regardless of coaching ability. Most head coaches have more assistants that they need anyway. So, if a staff member can't pull his own weight, the others will just have to take up the slack. It's just a matter of teamwork.
8. Act as the lone authority in discipline cases: Have no set judicial policy or uniform penalty code. Decide each case on its own merits and dispense justice as you see fit. Tell the coaches that every kid is different and each case must be dealt with individually. This will let the track coach know why his reserve pole vaulter was thrown off the team for drinking, while the all-state basketball center received only a warning for a similar offense.
9. Discuss your coach's flaws with anyone who'll listen: Parents, teachers, administrators, saloon cronies, other A.D.'s, and rival coaches are all potential audiences. Don't worry if your comments find their way back to the coach. Maybe they'll inspire him to work harder.
10. Show up in the locker room after a win, but never after a loss: You don't reward a loser. If you comfort a coach after a loss, he might get the idea that you tolerate losing. Coaches must be ever aware that winning is what athletics is all about.

10 Sure Ways for the Coach to Make the Faculty Hate Him

1. Complain about what you don't have: Demand that your budgetary and material needs be given priority over everything else. Make sure everyone knows that your problems are the only ones that count. This will endear you to the English teacher with no books and the science teacher with no test tubes.
2. Complain about your teaching load: Make it plain that teaching is merely a necessary evil that must be endured so

you can coach. Insist upon getting an hour off because of the time and pressure involved in coaching. Don't sympathize with the shop teacher with 45 students in a class designed for 25, or the sophomore class advisor who spends untold hours after school for little or no pay.

3. Never attend any faculty or union meetings: Gloat when other teachers trudge toward mandatory gatherings while you head for practice. Make sure they know that coaches are too important to be wasting time at meetings. Don't support any union activity unless it directly concerns your coaching position.
4. In the lunchroom or teacher's lounge, sit only with other coaches: Never talk about anything but sports. Dominate every conversation with opinions about the game, past or future. Show disdain for anyone who didn't see last night's game on TV. If ladies are present, make sure your language is salty enough to make them uncomfortable.
5. Psychoanalyze your players and their parents in front of other teachers: Go into detail about their faults and weaknesses. Also, downgrade students who aren't athletes. Teachers are always interested to learn why you consider their friends, neighbors, and pupils "bums, losers, and jerks."
6. Never volunteer for a job unless it's sports-related: Don't chaperone a dance, help on a candy sale, take tickets at a play, get involved in a class project, or do anything else not classified as "sports." Make everyone understand that athletics is the only school activity important enough to rate your concern.
7. Assign students sports-related tasks during another teacher's class period, and never ask permission beforehand. A note saying "he was with me" is sufficient. All teachers understand that folding uniforms is more important than listening to lectures.
8. Claim to be so nervous on game day that you can't teach: Beg for a movie about "anything that will fill up an hour." Or send all your classes to the library. Your professionalism will impress everyone.
9. Try to circumvent the eligibility rules: Don't focus on the spirit of the rule, but look for the technical loopholes. And make it known that athletes cannot fail your class no matter how hard they try.

10. Don't thank those who come to your games; complain about those who don't come: After all, everyone should shape his life around the schedule of your team. Teachers should realize that their job includes attending athletic contests, even if it means letting their classwork slide.

Stan Saplin's One Dozen (Not So Shrinking) Violets from NYU

No shrinking Violet himself, Stan Saplin worked for his alma mater, New York University, as Sports Information Director and Assistant to the President. He has also been a sportswriter (*New York Journal-American*) and Director of Public Relations for the New York Rangers. His list is in no special order.

1. Ken Strong
2. Howard Cosell
3. Neil Diamond
4. Sam Mele
5. Satch Sanders
6. Eddie Yost
7. Jack Lord
8. Ralph Branca
9. Carol Heiss
10. Dolph Schayes
11. Bob Pastor
12. Leslie MacMitchell

Hubert Mizell's 10 Most Prestigious College Football Coaching Jobs

Hubert Mizell is sports editor and columnist for the *St. Petersburg* (Fla.) *Times.*

1. Notre Dame
2. Southern California
3. Alabama
4. Oklahoma
5. Ohio State
6. Texas
7. Penn State
8. Michigan
9. Nebraska
10. Arkansas

Hubert Mizell's 7 Most Prestigious College Basketball Coaching Jobs

1. UCLA
2. Kentucky
3. North Carolina
4. Indiana
5. Notre Dame
6. Kansas
7. Duke

Abe Goteiner's Top 10 NAIA School Alumni

Abe Goteiner, a native New Yorker, is a former assistant publicity director for the National Association of Intercollegiate Athletics, headquartered in Kansas City, Mo. He became a proud proponent of the small colleges after spending four years at Doane College (enrollment: 600), in Crete, Neb. (population: 5,000). Says Goteiner: "The so-called 'big-time' colleges and universities don't have a monopoly on quality athletes. Over the years, a great many fine athletes have attended schools affiliated with the NAIA."

1. Ralph Boston, Tennessee A&I (track and field)
2. Lou Brock, Southern University (baseball)
3. Willie Davenport, Southern University-Baton Rouge (track and field)
4. Bruce Jenner, Graceland (track and field)
5. Jack Kemp, Occidental (football)
6. Earl "The Pearl" Monroe, Winston-Salem (basketball)
7. Bobby Morrow, Abilene Christian (track and field)
8. Walter Payton, Jackson State (football)
9. Willis Reed, Grambling (basketball)
10. Jack Sikma, Illinois Wesleyan (basketball)

George E. Killian's 10 Greatest Former Junior College Basketball Players Who Made the NBA

1. Spencer Haywood, Trinidad State JC, Colorado
2. Bob McAdoo, Vincennes University, Indiana
3. Larry Kenon, Amarillo JC, Texas
4. Artis Gilmore, Gardner-Webb JC, North Carolina
5. Freddie Brown, Burlington JC, Iowa
6. Nate Archibald, Arizona Western JC
7. Tom Henderson, San Jacinto College, Texas
8. Clarence "Foots" Walker, Vincennes University, Indiana
9. Ricky Sobers, College of Southern Idaho
10. John Johnson, Northwest CC, Wyoming

George E. Killian is Executive Director of the National Junior College Athletic Association.

Olympic decathlon champion Bruce Jenner on the victory stand at Montreal, with West Germany's Guido Kratschmer, silver, and Russia's Nikolai Avilov, bronze.

UPI

XVIII

By the Sea

James "Doc" Counsilman's 10 Greatest Men and 10 Greatest Women Swimmers of All Time

Coach at Indiana University for 23 years, and United States Olympic coach twice, Doc Counsilman is one of the foremost names in swimming. He agreed to make these selections with the disclaimer that his lists stop short of the 1980 Olympics, when newcomers appeared likely to crowd their way into the top 10.

MEN

1. Mark Spitz, United States—Winner of seven gold medals in 1972, he swam under Counsilman at Indiana.
2. Johnny Weissmuller, United States—He was, according to Counsilman, ahead of his time.
3. Roland Mathes, East Germany—A gold-medal winner in two successive Olympics.
4. Don Schollander, United States
5. Murray Rose, Australia
6. Brian Goodell, United States—A world record-holder for five years.

Johnny Weismuller won five Olympic gold medals in swimming.

UPI

7. Gary Hall, United States—Competed in three Olympics. Never won a gold medal, but held many world records.
8. Hironoshin Furuhashi, Japan—World War II prevented him from winning an Olympic medal.
9. John Naber, United States—A short, but spectacular career.
10. Jesse Vassallo, United States—Best of the current bunch.

WOMEN

1. Kornelia Ender, East Germany
2. Tracy Caulkins, United States
3. Dawn Fraser, Australia
4. Shane Gould, Australia
5. Eleanor Holm, United States
6. Chris von Saltza, United States
7. Debbie Meyer, United States
8. Ann Curtis, United States
9. Regneld Heger, Holland
10. Katherine Rawls, United States

Tom Hetzel's 10 Greatest Men and 10 Greatest Women Channel Swimmers of All Time

Channel swimming is a sport unto itself. Why do people swim the English Channel? Probably, as Sir Edmund Hillary said of climbing Mt. Everest, "because it's there," between Calais, France, and Dover, England, a distance of 20.6 nautical miles at its shortest point, but often more than twice that distance, depending on tidal conditions.

In the first 92 years after the first crossing in 1875, fewer than 100 people swam the Channel. Since 1967, more than 100 have crossed, bringing the number of swimmers who have crossed to 214 through 1979.

Tom Hetzel, who prepared this list, chose not to rate himself. Others would put him at the top of the list. He has the most crossings by an American (8), and has more relay crossings (6) than any swimmer, helping to establish six world records in the process. He was voted by the Channel Swimming Association as "the man who has done most for Channel swimming in the last 50 years." He coached James "Doc" Counsilman, who in 1979 became the oldest man to swim the Channel. Hetzel hopes to become the first to swim the Channel in the decades of the 60s, 70s, and 80s.

Tracy Caulkins, displays five gold medals and one silver from the 1978 world championships in Berlin.

UPI

MEN

1. Capt. Matthew Webb, England—The first ever to swim the English Channel, in 1875.
2. Kevin Murphy, England—The first to complete two double crossings of the Channel.
3. Henry Sullivan, United States—Had the longest solo success against the Channel, in 1923.
4. Edward Temme, England—The first to succeed in crossing in both directions, swimming from France to England in 1927, from England to France in 1934.
5. Jon Erikson, United States—The fastest two-way solo, 22 hours, six minutes, 1979.
6. Barry Watson, England—The fastest time from England to France, nine hours, 35 minutes, set in 1964.
7. Michael Read, England—The greatest number of crossings, 16. He has an advantage. He lives on the Channel and owns a boat.
8. Antonio Albertonto, Argentina—The first to do a two-way solo, 43 hours, 10 minutes, 1961.
9. James "Doc" Counsilman, United States—In 1979, at 58, the famed coach of Indiana University was the oldest man to swim the Channel.
10. Ted Erikson, United States—Held the record for the fastest double crossing, 30 hours, three minutes, until it was broken by his son, Jon.

WOMEN

1. Gertrude Ederle, United States—The first woman to swim across the Channel, 1926.
2. Florence Chadwick, United States—The first woman to cross from England to France. She made three crossings and has one world record.
3. Penny Lee Dean, United States—The fastest overall time, man or woman—7 hours, 40 minutes, 1978.
4. Cynthia Nicholas, Canada—The fastest two-way solo, 1979.
5. Stella Taylor, United States—Two crossings, and at 45 the oldest woman to swim the Channel.
6. Lynne Cox, United States—Two solo crossings, one world record.

Florence Chadwick after completion of her swim from England to France.
UPI

7. Greta Anderson, United States—Five solo crossings, one world record, and the only Olympic gold medal winner to cross the Channel.
8. Linda McGill, Australia—Three solo crossings, one world record.
9. Corrie Ebbelaar, Holland—One solo crossing, one world record, and two relay crossings, during which she helped establish four world records.
10. Rosemary George, England—The only English woman to swim the Channel twice. She lives in Dover.

Thomas C. Hardman's 10 Firsts and Foremosts of Water Skiing

Thomas C. Hardman, editor and publisher of the American Water Ski Association's official publication, *The Water Skier,* is also co-author of the book *Let's Go Water Skiing.*

1. First Water Skier—Although water skiing is considered by most to be a sport of recent vintage, the late Ralph Samuelson started it way back in 1922, on Lake Pepin near Lake City, Minn. Samuelson reasoned that if you could ski on snow, you should be able to do it on water. He finally proved his point, riding on two pine boards nine feet long and eight inches wide, which he had curved at the ends by boiling them in water.
2. Youngest Water Skier—Curt Chandler of Hollywood, Fla., learned to ski in the summer of 1979, at the age of 16 months.
3. Oldest Water Skier—Dr. J. C. McPheeters, president emeritus of Asbury College, in Wilmore, Ky., celebrated his 90th birthday in July of 1979 by going water skiing. McPheeters learned to ski at 73 and mastered the one-ski deep-water start at 79.
4. Youngest Nationals Competitor—Ricky McCormick, of Independence, Mo., entered his first National Water Ski Championships in 1960, when he had just turned eight. He was still at it in 1979, winning his third national open overall title in succession.

Ricky McCormick has won three national open overall championships.
American Water Ski Association

5. Oldest Nationals Competitor—Irene Horton, of Newberry Springs, Calif., competed in slalom in the 1974 Nationals at the age of 71. She had two children and three grandchildren competing in the same tournament.
6. Longest Water-Ski Jump—John Mondor, of Hollywood, Fla., leaped 187 feet off a six-foot ramp in a tournament at Tyler, Tex., in July of 1979. Charles R. Sligh, Jr., set the first national jumping record at Cypress Gardens, Fla., in 1947. His distance: 47 feet.
7. Best Slalom Score—58 buoys, a record held jointly by the LaPoint brothers, Kris and Bob, of Castro Valley, Calif. For the final four buoys scored consecutively at 36 miles an hour, the skiers were on an 11.25-meter line, 25 centimeters shorter than the distance from the path of the towboat to the buoys they were rounding.
8. Best Tricks Score—8,140 points, compiled by Patrice Martin, of Graslin, France, at the 1979 World Championships in Toronto, Canada.
9. Longest in 3-Event Competition—By 1979, Dr. Lew West, a Seattle dentist, had been competing in slalom, jumping, and tricks for 33 years.
10. Longest Non-Stop Water-Ski Run—Ray DeFir, of Portland, Ore., skied on a single ski for 1,000 miles in 33 hours and 27 minutes on the Columbia River in 1958.

The 10 Best Beach Volleyball Players and 5 Best Beach Volleyball Teams of All Time

Beach volleyball is largely a southern California athletic phenomenon. America's outstanding volleyball players have traditionally taken the summer off from indoor competition to play in doubles tournaments in the sun and sand of the dozens of beaches that dot the California coast. Today, the game is also played in Colorado, Florida, the Midwest, and along the eastern seaboard. Since its strictly amateur beginnings in the 1950s, the sport has grown to where winning players can pocket a good share of the over $50,000 in cash prizes available in various tournaments during the course of the summer.

THE 10 BEST PLAYERS

(Listed in Chronological Order of Competition)

1. Bernie Holtzman
2. Gene Selznick
3. Mike O'Hara
4. Mike Bright

5. Ron Lang
6. Ron Von Hagen
7. Larry Rundle
8. Henry Bergmann
9. Greg Lee
10. Jim Menges

THE 5 BEST TEAMS

(Listed in Chronological Order of Competition)

1. Bernie Holtzman-Gene Selznick
2. Mike Bright-Mike O'Hara
3. Ron Lang-Ron Von Hagen
4. Larry Rundle-Henry Bergmann
5. Greg Lee-Jim Menges

SOURCE: *Volleyball* magazine.

Donald Campbell astride his Bluebird, and his father, Sir Malcolm Campbell, in World War II, when he headed a British Military Police unit.
UPI

XIX

The Checkered Flag

Bob Cutter's 22 Famous Sons, 1 Daughter, 17 Brother Acts, 1 Half-Brother Act, and 2 Brother-Sister Acts in Auto Racing

Bob Cutter, who writes a syndicated column called "The Steering Column," has been covering automobiles and auto racing for more than a quarter of a century. He is co-author of *The Encyclopedia of Auto Racing Greats,* and author of *The Complete Book of Motorcycling* and *The Model Car Handbook.*

SONS

1. Mike Andretti—Everyone knows Mario, the Indy champ and second American to be World Driving Champion. But only go-kart fans know Mike, who started racing the low-slung, high-speed, sledlike vehicles in 1970, when he was 9. Soon, though, auto racing fans of all kinds may know the newest racing Andretti. He wants to be a world champ, like his dad.
2. Alberto Ascari—The first two-time, back-to-back World Driving Champion (1952–53) began racing motorcycles, graduated to cars in 1940, and was killed testing a car in 1957 at the age of 37. His father, Antonio, who raced Grand Prix cars from 1911 until 1925, was also 37 when he was killed in the French GP. Alberto's son, Tonino, tried racing, too, but never reached the level of his dad or grandfather.

3. Buddy Baker—Elzie Wylie Baker, Jr., to give him his full name. Racing since he was 17, in 1958, today he is a top-flight NASCAR driver, just like his father, Elzie, Sr., better known as Buck, a two-time NASCAR champion and former Greyhound bus driver.
4. Gary Bettenhausen—A championship (Indy) car racer of no mean talent, Gary started out in go-karts, but excelled in stock and sprint cars, as well as the open-cockpit Champ cars, just like his father, Melvin "Tony" Bettenhausen. Also known as the Tinsley Park Express, Tony was a USAC National Champion. Tough Tony raced from 1938 until 1951, when he was killed testing a friend's car. Gary has been racing professionally since 1961.
5. Merle Bettenhausen—Tony's other son, Merle, lost an arm in a 1972 race accident, and retired.
6. Geoff Brabham—He tires of being described as the son of three-time World Champion Jack Brabham, of Australia, but in 1979, the 27-year-old won his first big championship, the Robert Bosch/Volkswagen Gold Cup Super Vee title, and started racing in the Citicorp Canadian-American Challenge. Daddy began racing at 21, in 1947, and retired in 1970, steeped in honors and famed for his car-building as well as his racing expertise. Geoff only started racing in 1973, in Formula Ford. Daddy didn't encourage him, but didn't discourage him, either. The first father-son World Champion might be the result.
7. Donald Campbell—Technically, Donald wasn't a racing driver. He was a Land Speed Record (and Water Speed Record) driver, just like his father, Malcolm. World War I pilot Malcolm started racing cars in 1906 and didn't stop until 1935. He continued with speed boats for four more years, then retired, and died in 1948 of natural causes. Donald only picked up the mantle after his father's death, both on water and land, becoming the only man to set both LSR and WSR marks in the same year (1964). Donald was killed in 1967 when his speedboat disintegrated in a crash.
8. Pancho Carter—Father and son both were named Duane. The senior started racing in 1932, moved into the 1960s before concentrating on behind-the-scenes involvements in racing. By then, the younger Duane, universally called Pancho, was in action at Indy and other sprint, midget, and championship car tracks.

9. Lou Chinetti—Those who don't know him call the son of famed Ferrari impresario Luigi Chinetti "CoCo," a pet nickname of his father and his friends. But the younger Chinetti prefers Lou. Luigi has been one of Enzo Ferrari's best friends, from their Alfa Romeo days to the present. He drove in every LeMans between 1932 and 1953, winning three of the famed 24-hour battles. Lou has also driven at LeMans and other worldwide tracks, has been to Bonneville, and has designed cars as well as driven them. He also has one of the great model-car collections.
10. Al Holbert—Father Robert was one of the truly great American amateur racing drivers between 1951 and 1964, particularly in Porsches and Cobras. Son Al started racing Porsches, too, in 1971, and has tried his hand at everything from NASCAR stockers to ground-effects Canadian-American Challenge disguised six-seaters, as well as participating in the International Race of Champions. He was an IMSA champion.
11. Alan Jones—In 1979, Australia's stocky young man won more Grands Prix than anyone else, but he finished second in the point standing. In 1978, he was the CanAm Champion. In 1980, he was a favorite to contend for the World Driving Championship again. Bloodlines do tell. His father, Stan, was one of the great drivers who never left Down Under, but contented himself with blowing away local and visiting competition.
12. Stirling Moss—One of the greatest drivers in history despite never winning the World Driving Championship (194 victories in 466 starts), he was the son of a dentist-racing driver named Alfred. Lest you think dad was a low-level racer, be it known that Alfred made it into the Indianapolis 500 a couple of times in the 1920s, remarkable for a parttimer. In Britain, if you say "race driver" to the man on the street, most still will answer "Stirling Moss."
13. Johnny Parsons—Dad was always called Johnnie Parsons. He was USAC National Champion in 1949, won Indy the following year, and retired in 1959. Son Johnny has had a similar champ car career, though he has yet to win either the famed 500 or a national championship.
14. Larry Pearson—There may always be a Pearson in NASCAR racing. First was the father, David, also known as the Silver Fox, winner of more Grand National stock car races since he

began in 1952 than anyone except Richard Petty, and now there is a rising son-driver in the Grand National stock car world. Since there is also a younger Petty racing, the famed Pearson-Petty duels may last for another generation, at least, with new actors.

15. Skip Penske—He's only starting, but he's going to have the opportunity. Dad, Roger Penske, is the one-time race driver, race-car owner, track owner, race promoter, and automotive and financial genius. Dad drove from 1958 until 1965, then quit cold to take up other interests that have led his teams to Indy 500 victories, national championships, CanAm titles, Grand Prix racing, the works. It's nice to have a father like that, but it has its handicaps. "Do as I say, AND as I do."

16 and 17. Richard and Kyle Petty—They have to be an entry. Granddaddy was the legendary Lee Petty, Daddy is the even more legendary Richard Petty, and son—will he become a legend, too?—is Kyle. Lee was 35 before he ever raced at NASCAR, risking the family Buick. He never finished lower than sixth in his 12-year GN career, and won three NASCAR championships. But Richard is even better. Starting in 1959, he has become the winningest stock-car driver ever, both in total races and in championships (his latest in 1979). Son Kyle appears to have the makings. Like his daddy, he is having trouble finishing in his early career, but look at what Richard did later. And Kyle has several years' start on the old man (and almost a generation start on granddaddy). A Petty and NASCAR should still be in business at the turn of the next century.

18. Hans Stuck—Hans Stuck von Villiez raced nearly 40 years, starting with a class victory at age 24 and ending with a mountain championship at age 60. He raced Mercedes and Auto Union cars in the pre-World War II monster-Grand Prix era, BMWs after the war. The father died of natural causes in 1979. Son Hans also raced BMWs, now perhaps the classiest of all German cars, in the 1970s IMSA Camel GT Series, and made it into GP racing in a variety of cars. He even has tried a stock car. Like his father, he is tall and athletic, and looks less like a race driver than a soccer star or skier. Until you look in his eyes. As Bill France puts it, "He looks like a racer. He looks hungry for victory."

19. Bobby Unser, Jr.—Dad is the multi-time Indy winner and National champion in USAC/CART single-seaters, and son

of Jerry, Sr., who specialized in hill climbs. Bobby, Jr., is just getting started, but the Unser family breeds race drivers generation after generation, so Junior should get his chance. If he has the talent, he will win. The equipment and the backing will be his, but he will have to make it pay off.

20. Billy Vukovich—Dad was the Silent Serb of USAC racing, Bill Vukovich (born Vucerovich), who starred on U.S. tracks from 1937 until his death in 1955 at the Indy 500, which he had won the two previous years. Billy is not a "junior" (different middle name). He was 11 when his dad died, and 20 when he started racing professionally in 1964. He is a winner and a man in his own right.

21 and 22. Don and Bill Whittington—Daddy started in auto racing late in life, but R. D. influenced his sons to go into racing just as he had influenced them to make money. Reputed to be millionaires, the Whittingtons went to drivers' school, and within 16 months had shared a 24-hour race victory at prestigious LeMans. But their main racing is done in the high-powered IMSA Camel GT series, and in airplane racing.

DAUGHTER

1. Pat Moss—We mentioned Alfred's boy, Stirling. There's a daughter, too, who made her mark in auto competition. Pat wasn't a racer, but a rallyist, in the tough European fast-rallying school, like her mom. She married Sweden's premier rallyist, Erik Carlsson. A unique brother-sister-mother-father-brother-sister-husband act.

BROTHERS

1. Bobby and Donnie Allison—Two NASCAR stockcar aces competing against one another. Two years separate these Floridians, and in Bobby's favor are many more victories. But on any given day, each is the equal of the other, and many door-to-door battles have thrilled southern fans through the years.
2. Art and Walt Arfons—Not race-car drivers, but Land Speed record-holders. Of the pair, Art (younger by nine years) was the dominant one in his famed Green Monster cars. They worked together, then split and went their separate ways, first in drag racing, then in the LSR business. Walt hired drivers; Art continued to drive his own jet-powered cars.

3. Mario and Aldo Andretti—Twins. Aldo matched Mario feat-for-feat until an accident ended his career, although he still follows brother Mario's soaring fortunes closely. Nothing need be said about the talented and terrific Mario Andretti. The name is enough to remind people of his feats.
4. Merle and Gary Bettenhausen—Sons of Tough Tony, their story is told in the father-son section.
5. Georges and Andre Boillot—There were three Boillot brothers, although only these two raced cars. Georges was a pre-World War I star in Peugeots, then died in the French Air Service over Verdun. Andre started racing in 1919, won the famed Targa Florio, raced at Indianapolis three times, and continued racing until 1931.
6. Foggy and Buddy Calloway—From 1927 until 1938, these Georgians raced with the predecessor NASCAR stockcar groups, then retired to Miami. They were as famed for their singing prowess as for their driving, and neither pastime was bad.
7. Louis, Gaston, and Arthur Chevrolet—Eight years separated these three French-born racing brothers who gained greatest fame in the United States, starting with Louis in 1905. Arthur won his class in the first race ever held at the Indy Speedway (not the 500) in 1909. It was Louis who started what became the Chevrolet Car Company, and he was also active in early aviation. Arthur split off to move into boats.
8. Sam and Miles Collier—Not the famed recluses, these Collier brothers were amateur sportsmen who had much to do with popularizing sports cars in post-World War II America and with the founding of the Sports Car Club of America. Sam was the more active driver of the two, and was killed in 1950 in a racing accident. Miles died in 1954 of natural causes.
9. Maurice and Henri Farman—Born in France, the three Farman brothers were actually English. Only two raced, first Maurice, then Henri (also known as Henry), beginning in the late 1890s. Maurice switched to less dangerous airplane flying and founded his own company, which supplied the French in World War I. He died in 1964, at the age of 96.
10. Emerson and Wilson Fittipaldi—Wilson was the first of the Brazilian brothers to race (go-karts and motorcycles), but Emerson was the more talented behind the wheel. Wilson retired to help his brother eventually win the World Driving Championship in 1972, and Emerson continues to this day to

make his own car designs. At the time he won his title, he was the youngest man to accomplish that feat.

11. Tim and Fonty Flock—There were four brothers, but these two made their marks as stock-car stars, even before there was a NASCAR. Tim was the younger. He started racing in 1947 and won a Grand National crown in 1952. Fonty had been racing since 1940, and even before that, had been running moonshine through police roadblocks. More or less retired by the late 1950s, Fonty turned to things like creating a fan-club program for NASCAR. He died in 1972 after a long illness.
12. Algernon and Kenelm Guinness—Algy was a turn-of-the-century, seat-of-the-pants driver, Bill a scientific driver who continued into the 1920s. Yes, they were part of that Irish stout family, as well as early racing pioneers. The younger Bill died in 1937, Algy in 1954.
13. Carlo, Alfieri, and Ernesto Maserati—There were three other brothers, and two of them were also involved in cars, but only Carlo (before World War I) and Ernesto and Alfieri (in the 1920s and 1930s) raced. Of the three, Alfieri probably was the best. The group founded a car company that was sold off in 1947. Then they founded another company called OSCA.
14. Pedro and Ricardo Rodriguez—Ricardo was the younger of the two Mexican brothers, and was killed in 1962 while practicing for his native Grand Prix. He was 20. Pedro, two years older, started racing in 1957, the same season as the 15-year-old Ricardo did, and he lasted and prospered in international racing, including the Grand Prix circus. Considered one of the great endurance drivers of all time, he was killed in an Interserie (European version of the CanAm) race at Norisring, Germany, in 1971. He was 31.
15. Ian and Jody Scheckter—Ian has confined almost all of his racing to South Africa, the brothers' homeland, but Jody moved to Europe and worked his way up to World Driving Champion in 1979, after a hairy early career in which he regularly was expected to kill himself due to his all-out, sliding style.
16. Al, Bobby, and Jerry Unser—Jerry, Sr., raced, and so did two uncles, so it was natural for three of the four Unser boys (the fourth had multiple sclerosis, so he raced only boats) to go into auto racing. Jerry, Jr., was killed at Indy in 1959, so it was left to older Bobby and baby Al (five years younger) to

Defending Indy 500 champion Bobby Unser *(left)* with brother Al, before the 1976 Indy.

UPI

carry on the family tradition, which they did with a vengeance. Between winning Indy five times between them, and several national championships, they have also dominated USAC/CART racing for long stretches at a time, despite the presence of people like Foyt, Sneva, and others.

17. Don and Bill Whittington—Their story is told in the father-son section.

THE HALF-BROTHERS

1. Johnny Parsons and Pancho Carter—Johnnie Parsons and Duane Carter, Sr., were married to the same woman at different times, and each fathered a son by the same woman, making Johnny Parsons and Pancho Carter half-brothers, a situation unique in auto racing (and most other sports). Each son became a sprint, midget, and championship car racer in USAC/CART. Bill Stern would have loved this one.

BROTHER-SISTER

1. Trevor and Anita Taylor—Trev was a contemporary of Jimmy Clark, starting in 1955 with sports cars, then moving to single-seaters, all the way up to the Grand Prix series in 1960. Later, he concentrated on Formula 5000, but never achieved the status of Clark. Anita, a raving beauty, raced from 1961 until 1967 in so-called "saloon" cars, or more or less stock European sedans. She retired only because she believed a married woman should not race cars.
2. Stirling and Pat Moss—Certainly the most talented brother-sister act in auto competition ever, their story is told in the sons and daughters section.

Tony Dorsett, now a Dallas Cowboy, won the 1976 Heisman Trophy when he played for the University of Pittsburgh.

UPI

XX

Ho-Hum

Blackie Sherrod's 18 Most Overrated Things in American Sports

As a sports columnist for the *Dallas Times-Herald,* Blackie Sherrod is not overrated.

1. The Heisman Trophy
2. The Pro Bowl
3. Sonny Liston
4. America's Cup
5. Reggie Jackson
6. The Ryder Cup
7. Ilie Nastase
8. Teofilo Stephenson
9. Duane Thomas
10. The Minnesota Vikings' Purple People Eaters
11. Silky Sullivan
12. Shirley May France
13. Olympic gymnastics
14. Golf gallery deportment
15. TV monitors as the answer to NFL officiating woes
16. Billy Martin's managerial genius
17. Sugar Ray Leonard
18. Baseball all-star balloting

Ray Fitzgerald's 10 Most Boring Moments in Sports

1. Kickoffs into the end zone
2. Icing the puck
3. Timeouts near the end of one-sided basketball games
4. One-sided basketball games
5. Intentional walks
6. Baseball rain delays
7. TV commercial timeouts
8. Carlton Fisk between pitches while batting
9. Stalling in college basketball
10. Howard Cosell playing God

SOURCE: *Boston Globe.*

Jay Simon's 10 Biggest Bores (Living or Dead) in Sports History

For the past seven years, Jay Simon has been editor of *Golf Digest*. Prior to that, he was sports editor of the *Daily Oklahoman* and sports information director at the University of Kansas. He says he can be completely objective about his list since he barely knew any of his bores personally. His list is alphabetical, because it was too boring to rate the bores.

1. George Allen
2. Avery Brundage
3. Jimmy Connors
4. Howard Cosell
5. Charles O. Finley
6. Woody Hayes
7. Bowie Kuhn
8. Adolph Rupp
9. Jimmy "the Greek" Snyder
10. Harry Wismer

XXI

A Mixed Bag

Gerald Dumas' 9 Rules of Etiquette for the Well-Mannered Runner

Gerald Dumas writes and draws "Sam and Silo," a King Features comic strip. He has drawn for the *New Yorker,* and is the author of *An Afternoon in Waterloo Park.* He has twice won the Connecticut four-wall handball championship, and reports he runs five miles in 36 minutes.

1. If someone at a cocktail party tells you how nicely gaunt and fit you look, do not put down your Perrier water and launch into an account of your daily 10-mile stint. No one wants to hear about your will power. Or even your shin splints. If you are a male runner talking to a woman, glance appreciatively at her cheek bones and ask her what her day was like. If you are talking to a funeral director or a man who fixes driveways, say thank you and walk away.
2. Female runners and male runners should not gravitate to one another in one corner of the room, laughing privately at dirty running jokes while freezing out outsiders. Welcome others, even those who are in good shape through frequent participation in another sport. It won't be easy, but you will be rewarded in heaven

3. At sit-down dinner parties, eat meagerly, but try to take over the conversation so you won't finish long before everyone else. Nothing is worse than a runner sitting around with an empty plate, making everyone else feel guilty. Do not occupy leftover time by pretending two of your fingers are a little man running across the tablecloth.
4. Try not to look smug. This is a widespread sin and will be difficult to eradicate. A lone runner's face on a suburban road contains equal parts of pain, pride, gritty will, and narrow-minded smugness. It is, in short, a terrible sight. Better to affect an air of mildly bewildered artlessness; your face should say, "Goodness, I certainly hope all this is going to do me some good." Upon seeing such a face, drivers may think twice before trying to bounce you over the ditch and into the mailboxes.
5. At summer parties, always wear a jacket. Do not show up with just your East Quogue Roadrunners shirts on with the poor cartoon of a bird on it. No one wants to see that, and no one wants to see how thin your arms are, either.
6. Avoid chafing. Use plenty of powders and oils on your underarms and inner thighs so you will not offend people by standing in a crouch with your feet wide apart and your arms akimbo. Readers have often wondered why superheroes like Spiderman and Superman have only one stance—the crouch, with arms raised and spread, the ankles 12 feet apart. It's because they are miserably chafed from their heroic exertions. If you get chafed anyway and find that you must stand in the heroic stance, at least wear a cape.
7. In a restaurant, if you are bothered by smoke from an adjoining table, do not explain that you are a distance runner and that smoke does not fit in with your life-style. Life is too short for that. Simply say, "Bye, bye, naughty cigarette," and pluck it from the smoker's lips. All etiquette books now say this is perfectly acceptable. It is also the one time when it is all right to look smug. If the offending smoker is large and rises menacingly from the table, do wind sprints until you are around the corner.
8. Distance running carries with it heartache, agony, pain, and suffering. In a social situation, if you find that you are about to expound on the glory and wonder of it all, change the subject, even if it gives you a stitch in the side.

9. When running on narrow, twisting roads, do not yell "Slow down!" at a driver who suddenly finds you in line with his right front headlight. Remember, you knew he was coming, but to him you are quite a surprise. If the driver is elderly, allay his fears by stopping completely. If necessary, lean against a tree, wave cheerily, and run merrily in place.

SOURCE: *New York Times.*

Ron Guidry's 3 Favorite Places to Hunt

In the summer, Yankee left-hander Ron Guidry hunts batters with his blazing fastball and wicked slider, having struck out 477 of them in two seasons, 1978 and 1979. During the fall and winter, Guidry hunts different game. As soon as the baseball season ends, he heads for his home in Lafayette, La., grabs his shotgun, and catches up on his other passion, hunting. He likes the peace and quiet after a long, hard season, preferring to hunt for ducks, and also preferring to stay in the Louisiana country he knows best.

1. Grand Chenier, Cameron Parish, La. (near the Rockefeller Preserve)—duck hunting.
2. Lake Arthur—In the Louisiana bayou country, near where he was born in Lafayette, La. Guidry takes his whole family here to go duck hunting.
3. Ron Guidry's Place—This is a secret place in Louisiana where Guidry goes hunting for woodchuck, and he's not about to give away his secret. "Only one other person knows about it," says Guidry. "That's Grandfather Gus, who taught me to hunt when I was a kid."

Roy Blount's 5 Best Airports

In his travels as a freelance writer, Roy Blount has flown in and out of literally hundreds of airports.

1. Atlanta—A five-minute cab ride to the Flying Pig (out toward Hapeville), where you can get honest barbecue. You will need to be fortified with honest barbecue for the walk to your gate, which is farther away than Hapeville. This is also the only major airport where you can buy a big bag of speckled grits for no more than you would pay for the same-sized bag of pearls anywhere else.

2. Nashville (home of the Vanderbilt Commodores)—Only airport where you can buy country-music trade and gossip publications. You might see Roy Acuff.
3. Tampa—Everybody in the Tampa-St. Petersburg area says this is the finest airport facility in the world. Personally, I would rather have $2.50 in the sorriest beer joint in the world than $250 in the finest airport facility, but if you have to be in an airport facility, it might as well be the world's finest.
4. Pittsburgh—Good soft ice cream. A vaguely funky—by airport standards—coffee shop. You might see Billy Conn.
5. LaGuardia—An easy place to steal luggage.

SOURCE: *Inside Sports* magazine.

Minnesota Fats' 10 Best Pre-1950 and 10 Best Modern Pool Players

Rudolf Walter Wanderone, a product of New York City, says he hustled craps on the George Washington Bridge when it was being built. His subsequent career has made him a legend as Minnesota Fats, the world's most celebrated pool shark. "I'm the greatest pool player who ever lived," he confesses. "Pool is the toughest racket of all. Even Willie Mosconi, Ralph Greenleaf, and all the other great ones couldn't make a living out of pool alone and had to work. But I never worked a day of my life."

Present company excluded, Fats calls Mosconi and Greenleaf the greatest of all, but he wouldn't single one over the other. His listings are alphabetical. Regarding the modern players, he says: "Toss a coin. They're all great, each a queen for a day. I'm the only king."

1900 THROUGH THE LATE 1940S

1. George Clark
2. Irving Crane
3. Alfredo D'Orio
4. Ralph Greenleaf
5. Willie Hoppe
6. Tom Houston
7. Jimmy Moore
8. Andrew Ponzi
9. Erwin Rudolph
10. Andrew St. Jean

1950 TO THE PRESENT

1. Paul Brienza
2. Danny Gartner (Young Greenleaf)
3. Buddy Hall
4. Allen Hopkins
5. Larry Hubbard

Minnesota Fats is a legend on the green of the pool table. *Busch*

Jackie Gleason gives some pointers to Willie Mosconi. *UPI*

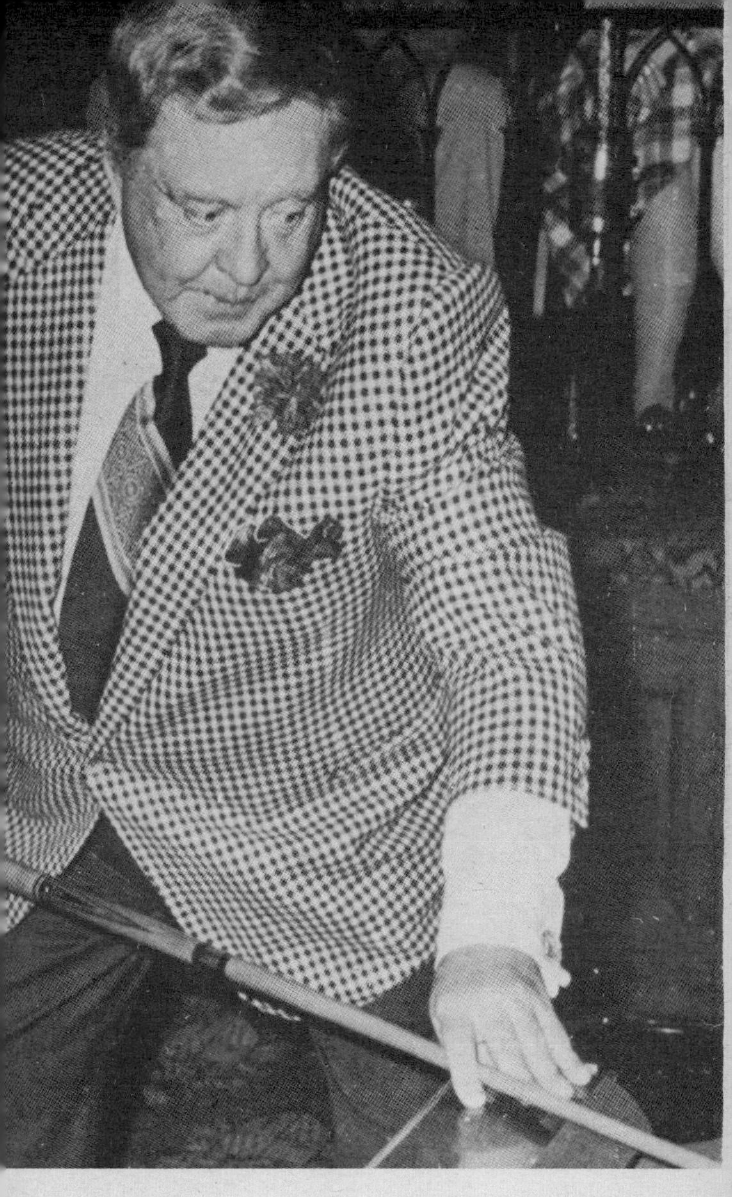

6. Peter Margo
7. Ray Martin
8. Jim Mataya
9. Steve Mizerak
10. Willie Mosconi

Minnesota Fats' 5 Greatest Celebrity Pool Players

1. Fred Astaire
2. Peter Falk
3. Jackie Gleason
4. Dean Martin
5. Omar Sharif

Fats notes: "They're in no particular order. I don't get to see or play them often. Usually on television it's just one rack, 30 minutes. I got a big kick out of meeting Sharif. It was on a movie set and he told Dick Stockton [the announcer], 'I'd give my life to meet Minnesota Fats.' And Dick introduced us. You know, he's a great bridge player, too."

Pat McDonough's 5 Super Southpaws of Bowling

Veteran sportswriter Pat McDonough is the publisher of a bowling newspaper, *The Sports Reporter,* and is the author of dozens of books and magazine articles on bowling. Says McDonough: "Are left-handers at a disadvantage in bowling as they are in golf? The answer is an unequivocal yes and no. Because of the need for dressing bowling lanes and because of the preponderance of right-handed bowlers, a lone southpaw among 10 league bowlers on a pair of lanes will find his conditions show little change during the course of a league session. But the amount of action on the right-hand side of the lane causes the dressing to be dispersed, with the resultant change from an oily condition to a dry situation. So the right-hander must adjust. If conditions are difficult to start with on the left side, they will stay that way, and vice versa. Whereas the right-handers find changing conditions sometimes for the better, sometimes for the worse."

1. Earl Anthony—The most successful pro bowler—first to win 30 titles, first to win $700,000—is a left-hander. He overtook Hall of Famer Dick Weber, who has been winning pro titles since the inception of the organization, in 1959. Earl can do so many things with angles, changes in ball speed, etc., that many times he can score on lanes that thwart other left-handers.

Earl Anthony, king of the left-handers. *UPI*

2. Dave Davis—Dave was the first southpaw ever to be named Bowler of the Year. He earned the accolade in 1967. His 18 titles are surpassed by only five other pros. He was fourth to top $500,000 in PBA earnings.
3. Johnny Petraglia—This Brooklyn native set a season's earnings record in 1971 with more than $85,000. He has won 12 pro titles and more than $400,000 in PBA competition.
4. Bill Allen—The first Super Southpaw. In the 1960s, he was annually the top-earning southpaw, bagging 13 titles. A fantastic clutch performer.
5. Mike McGrath—His 10 titles between 1965 and 1973 included two national championships and the U.S. Open. He was the leading earner in 1970, one of four left-handers who have earned this distinction in 20 years of PBA.

Milt Roth's 10 Greatest Jai-Alai Players Ever to Perform in the United States

Milt Roth has been associated with jai-alai for the past 20 years, as public relations director of Miami Jai-Alai. He was recently named president of the Frontons, in Daytona Beach and Melbourne, Florida. His list includes only the best players to perform in the United States. Adds Roth: "No list of jai-alai greats would be complete without the names Erdoza Menor, known as 'El Fenomeno,' and Joseph Apesteguy, known as 'Chiquito de Cambo.' They never made it to the United States, but their feats are legendary."

1. Guillermo Amuchastegui—The Babe Ruth of jai-alai.
2. Pedro Mir—He did it all.
3. Piston 1 (Estanislau Maiztegui)—Perfected the carom shot.
4. Francisco Churruca—King of the modern-day backcourt. Could be the all-time greatest.
5. Fernando Orbea—Classic front-courter.
6. Jose Luis Salsamendi—A master in the front court.
7. Ignacio Echeverria—The most devastating server the game has produced.
8. Jose Egurbidi—Right up there with the best.
9. Bolivar (Jose A. Illoro)—Modern superstar.
10. Joey Cornblit—An American who is revolutionizing the game.

Southpaw Babe Ruth loved to bowl; while former New York University and New York Giant footballer Ken Strong looks on, the Babe checks his score with Pat McDonough, bowling scribe and publisher.

Pat McDonough Collection

Phyllis Hollander's 10 Champion Sports Mothers

As more and more women are finding it possible to have careers as athletes, it became inevitable that there would be those who would combine motherhood with their dedication to sport. Phyllis Hollander, senior editor at Associated Features, is the author of *American Women in Sports* and *100 Greatest Women in Sports.*

1. Mary Bacon: The jockey rode in three consecutive races one day before admitting herself to the hospital where her daughter, Suzy, was born. Five years later, in 1974, she was rated among the Top Ten Jockeys at Aqueduct in New York, along with such stand-out male riders as Ron Turcotte, Jorge Velasquez, Eddie Maple, and Angel Cordero, Jr. She had ridden over 300 winners in her startling career, including New York's first all-woman Daily Double with Joan Phipps.
2. Fanny Blankers-Koen: Known as "the Flying Housewife," she was 30 years old with two children when she won a record four Olympic gold medals in track and field at London in 1948.
3. Olga Fikotova Connolly: Winner of the 1956 Olympic gold medal in the discus throw, she achieved a record of another kind by competing in the Munich Games in 1972 when she was the mother of four.
4. Margaret Smith Court: Australia's greatest woman tennis player, who amassed a career record of 66 Big Four victories including a Grand Slam in 1970, was a mother when she won the U.S. Open and 17 other major tournaments in 1973. After the birth of her second child, in 1975, she returned to the circuit, where she piled up $105,646 in earnings.
5. Nina Kuscsik: The first woman champion of the 26-mile, 385-yard Boston Marathon, she was the mother of three when she crossed the finish line in 1972, ahead of 800 male and eight other women runners in the time of 3.08:58.
6. Marion Ladewig: The first woman winner of the Bowling Proprietors Association of America all-star title, in 1949, she was a 50-year-old grandmother of five when she won her last major tournament, the World Invitational in 1965.
7. Floretta McCutcheon: When she defeated the legendary bowling champion, Jimmy Smith, by a three-game total of 704–687, she was the gray-haired mother of a college-age daughter.

Pedro Mir played jai-alai in his earliest days in the Basque region of Spain.

Miami Jai-Alai

5

1956 Olympic gold medalist Olga Fikotova Connolly threw the discus at Munich as the mother of four. *UPI*

8. Galina Prozumenshikova Stepanova: Russia's 1964 champion breast-stroker became the only known Olympic swimmer to make a medal-winning comeback after childbirth when she took the 100-meter silver medal and 200-meter bronze at the 1972 Munich Games.
9. Margaret Osborne du Pont: Married in 1947, this superb tennis player held a longevity record among women by ranking among the top ten 14 times between 1938 and 1958. As No. 1 and U.S. national champion in 1948–1950, du Pont was one of those relatively few players to win major tournaments after the birth of her son.
10. Glenna Collett Vare: Winner of the U.S. Golf Association amateur championship five times (1922, 1925, 1928, 1929, 1930), she made it No. 6 in 1935, when she was the 32-year-old mother of two.

Mary Bacon, mother of a Suzy, has had more than 300 winners. *UPI*

Motherhood didn't keep Margaret Smith Court from successfully swinging her racquet on the championship circuit. *UPI*

Bert Smith's 10 Greatest Cricket Players of All Time

Bert Smith is president of Cricket Classics, Inc., which has promoted the sport in the United States.

1. Sir Garfield Sobers, West Indies
2. Keith Miller, Australia
3. Sir Don Bradman, Australia

4. Sir Learie Constantine, West Indies
5. George Headley, West Indies
6. Len Hutton, England
7. Sir Frank Worrell, West Indies
8. Vinood Mancad, India
9. Richie Benaud, Australia
10. Dennis Compton, England

Smith adds: "Gary Sobers is without peer in the history of cricket, the greatest all-arounder ever to have graced the game. A devastating batsman, a bowler of world class in two styles, and of Test class in a third, the most interesting captain in modern cricket, and a magnificent fielder both close to the wicket and deep.

"His achievements are unbelievable. They include a world record tally of 7,627 runs in Test cricket, the highest-ever not outs, 365, against Pakistan in 1958, and the time against Glamorgan in 1966 when he hit six sixes, the only time that has been achieved in Test cricket."

George Gipe's 10 Favorite Sports Oddities

George Gipe, author of *The Great American Sports Book*, is a freelance writer whose articles have appeared in *American Heritage, Mad* magazine, and *Sports Illustrated.*

1. In an unusual statistical freak on August 18, 1910, Brooklyn and Pittsburgh (National League) played an 8–8 tie baseball game in which each team had a total of 38 at bats, 13 hits, 12 assists, two errors, five strikeouts, three walks, one hit batsman, and one passed ball.
2. In December, 1933, the basketball squad of John Tarleton College (Texas) lost to San Angelo Junior College, 27–26. Tarleton then proceeded to win 86 consecutive games before losing on February 2, 1938, to San Angelo Junior College, once again by the score of 27–26.
3. In the 1935 football game between Northwestern and Notre Dame, the Irish had a player named William Shakespeare. Not to be outdone, Northwestern's right end was named Henry Wadsworth Longfellow. Early in the "Battle of the Bards," Shakespeare was instrumental in the Irish taking a 7–0 lead, but in the fourth quarter, Longfellow made a sensational catch of a 14-yard pass to tie the game. Northwestern then went on to win, 14–7.

4. On June 19, 1973, Pete Rose of the Cincinnati Reds and Willie Davis of the Dodgers both got their 2,000th career hits. Rose collected a single against the Giants and Davis a home run against the Braves.
5. On December 18, 1937, a pair of Eskimo football teams of King Island, Alaska, were preparing for the New Year's Day Ice Bowl game. They had decided to practice on a huge ice floe near the village, because of its convenient shape and flatness, but before the teams could assemble, a brisk wind blew the field away.
6. In 1922, between the morning and afternoon games of a Memorial Day doubleheader, Max Flack of the Chicago Cubs and Cliff Heathcote of the St. Louis Cardinals were traded for each other. They played one game for each team on the same day.
7. In 1945, a horse named Never Mind II refused a jump during a steeplechase and was taken back to the paddock by his jockey. Upon arriving there, however, the jockey was told that all the other horses had been disqualified or fallen. The jockey, therefore, took Never Mind II back on the track and circled the course alone. The total winning time—including that used to walk the horse to the paddock and back—was 11 minutes, 28 seconds for the two-mile race, which is normally completed in four minutes.
8. In 1901, a promoter named Henri Deutsch decided to introduce a new wrinkle for bullfighting fans by pitting a bull against a matador riding in a car. The contest actually took place at Bayonne, France, with the bullfighter, Ledesma, waving to the crowd from the passenger's seat of a 12-horsepower Peugeot driven by a chauffeur. The bull turned tail and ran, however, causing some of the crowd to laugh and the rest to shout angry epithets at Monsieur Deutsch. The promoter presumably took his money and also ran.
9. Following an Army touchdown in the 1949 football game against Fordham, cadet placekicker Jack Mackmull successfully kicked the extra point. Army was penalized for unsportsmanlike conduct, however, and the ball was placed on the 17-yard line. Mackmull once again made the kick, but Army was again assessed 15 yards. Mackmull's third try was wide, but this time a Fordham player was charged with an infraction, giving Mackmull a fourth chance. He missed once

again. And once again Fordham was offside. Mackmull's fifth attempt for the point-after was finally made from the 18-yard line.

10. In November, 1938, Col. William Preston Lane, 87, the last surviving member of the Princeton team that had played Rutgers in the first Intercollegiate football game in America, passed away. In the 1869 contest, Rutgers won by a score of 6–4. There followed nearly seven decades during which Rutgers failed to repeat the victory over Princeton, the drought ending only after Lane died.

Ginny Akabene's 13 All-Time Women's Squash Champions

Ms. Akabene is the new president of the women's division of the United States Squash Racquets Association. She says: "Since I am fairly new to squash and not familiar with the players before the 1970s, and especially since squash has never received a great deal of publicity and, therefore, the national champions have never received their due in terms of recognition, I have chosen to compile a list of those women squash players having won the most national championships."

1.	Jane Stauffer	14
2.	Gretchen Spinance	12
3.	Bunny Vosters	11
	Peggy Carrott	11
	Betty Constable	11
6.	Jeanne Classen	10
7.	Barbara Hunter	8
8.	Edith Beatty	7
	Goldie Edwards	7
10.	Anne Page	6
	Joyce Davenport	6
	Weezie Manly-Power	6
	Fran Bottger	6

10 Points to Keep in Mind When Officiating Sports at Any Level

1. Be Competitive: The players give maximum effort, so should you. Tell yourself, "I'm not going to let this game get away

from me. I am better than that." You are hired to make the calls that control the game. Make them.

2. Have Your Head on Right: Don't think your striped shirt grants you immunity from having to take a little criticism. It's part of officiating. Plan on it. Successful officials know how much to take. Ask one when you get the chance.
3. Don't Be a Tough Guy: If a coach is on your back but not enough to warrant a penalty, then stay away from him (or her). This is especially true during time-outs. Standing near an unhappy coach, just to "show him" will only lead to further tensions. Some officials develop irritating characteristics. Don't be one of them.
4. Get Into the Flow of the Game: Each game is different. Good officials can feel this difference. Concentrate on the reactions of the players. Take note if the tempo of the game changes. A ragged game calls for a different style of officiating than a smooth one.
5. Don't Bark: If you don't like to be shouted at, don't shout at someone else. Be firm with a normal relaxed voice. This technique will do wonders in helping you to reduce the pressure. Shouting indicates a loss of control—not only of one's self, but also of the game.
6. Show Confidence: Cockiness has absolutely no place in officiating. You want to exude confidence. Your presence should command respect from the participants. As in any walk of life, appearance, manner, and voice determine how you are accepted. Try to present the proper image.
7. Forget the Fans: As a group, fans usually exhibit three characteristics—ignorance of the rules, highly emotional partisanship, and delight in antagonizing the officials. Accepting this fact will help you ignore the fans, unless they interrupt the game or stand in the way of you doing your job.
8. Answer Reasonable Questions: Treat coaches and players in a courteous way. If they ask you a question reasonably, answer them in a polite way. If they get your ear by saying, "Hey, ref, I want to ask you something," and then start telling you off, interrupt and remind them of the reason for the discussion. Be firm, but relaxed.
9. Choose Your Words Wisely: Don't obviously threaten a coach or player. This will only put them on the defensive. More important, you will have placed yourself on the spot. If you feel a situation is serious enough to warrant a threat,

then it is serious enough to penalize, without invoking a threat. Obviously, some things you say will be a form of threat, but using the proper words can make it subtle.

10. Stay Cool: Your purpose is to establish a calm environment for the game. Nervous or edgy officials are easily spotted by fans, coaches, and players alike. Avidly chewing gum, pacing around, or displaying a wide range of emotions prior to or during a game will serve to make you seem vulnerable to pressure.

SOURCE: *Referee* magazine.

Satch Furman's 10 Best (or Worst) Promotions

Andy "Satch" Furman, who some say has only 46 cards in his deck, was director of publicity and promotions for the Fort Lauderdale Strikers of the North American Soccer League. He came to the Strikers from Oral Roberts University, where he was sports information director and a legend in his own time. At ORU, he wanted to depart by letting all Indians in free for the game with the Oklahoma City Chiefs.

"I'll stand at the door and be able to spot the Indians," said Furman.

"How?" someone asked.

"That's one way," said Furman.

The promotion never got off the ground. Neither did Furman's idea for letting all girls with auburn hair in free for the Auburn game and all Satan worshipers in free for the game with the DePaul Demons.

1. Escape Night: This one never came off. The idea was to have a Houdini-type performer chained inside a box underwater. He was to escape or drown trying, either alternative being OK with Furman. In honor of the occasion, all ex-convicts would be admitted to the game free. "Not too much has been done for ex-cons lately, do you think?" said Furman.
2. The Great Horse Race: In order to validate defender Colin Fowles' claim that he is the fastest player in the NASL, Furman arranged a race between Fowles and a horse named Striker Liker. The horse won, but he was running on his home turf at Pompano Park.

3. Strike Night: This was a two-part promotion. First, the Striker players lived up to their name by going on strike. Then Furman announced that in the future, all workers on strike would be admitted to the Strikers' home games free.
4. Goldfish-Appreciation Night: The first 1,000 kids to the game were given free goldfish. Furman was hoping to have a goldfish-eating contest at halftime, but team officials would not permit this. The promotion was in honor of National Goldfish Day.
5. Dentist Night: All dentists were admitted free when the Strikers played the Vancouver Whitecaps.
6. Grandmother's Day: On Mother's Day, all grandmothers were admitted free if they were accompanied by a grandchild. In reply to the skeptics who believed some little old ladies would borrow fake grandkids for the game, Furman replied: "If we can't trust the grandmothers of America, who can we trust?"
7. Marriage Day: This is a proposed promotion. Any couple willing to get married on the field at halftime will see the game free. "If I can't find a couple who wants to get married," said Furman, "maybe there's a couple that wants to get divorced."
8. If-the-Shoe-Fits Night: When Striker Ray Hudson lost one of his sandals at the beach, Furman offered a reward. Anyone returning the sandal would receive a pair of tickets to the next home game. But first, Hudson would have to try on the sandal to see if it fit. No one showed up to claim the reward.
9. Phone-Book Day: Furman's first project after arriving in Fort Lauderdale was to call everyone in the Fort Lauderdale phone book and invite them to a soccer game. He got through the Fs before giving up.
10. Hypnotist Week: When the Strikers were in an early-season losing streak, Furman called on a psychoanalyst to counsel the players. Dr. Richard Gerson, who knew Furman from Brooklyn, responded, and the Strikers won their next game against Toronto. Dr. Gerson received a pair of tickets for his efforts.

SOURCE: *Tulsa Tribune*

A List of Lists for *The Book of Sports Lists #3*

Erich Segal's 10 Favorite Marathoners
Jerry Della Femina's 10 Ad Campaigns "I'd Most Like to Do with Athletes"
Joe Foss' 10 Favorite Places to Hunt
Mike Burke's 10 Most Daring Athletes in the OSS
Lou Miller's 10 Humans and Horses I Taught to Breathe
Sonny Werblin's 10 Greatest Sports Promoters
Bill Veeck's 10 Greatest Promotions
Bobby Orr's 10 Toughest Goalies
Michael Gartner's 10 Greatest Sports Figures from the *Wall Street Journal*
Herb Schnall's 10 Sports Books I Have Turned Down
Arlene Francis' 10 Most Beautiful Horses
Bob Hope's 10 Best and 10 Worst Golfers of All Time
Jackie Gleason's 10 Greatest Pool Sharks
Paul Newman's 10 Most Challenging Auto Race Tracks
Woody Allen's 10 Favorite Manhattan Street Games
Tiny Tim's 10 Favorite Athletic Heroes
Morganna's 10 Baseball Players I'd Most Like to Kiss Out on the Field